Code with C

The Beginner's Journey

SHRAVAN GEERLAPALLY

Copyright © 2024

All rights reserved.

ISBN: 9798346461630

DEDICATION

This book is dedicated to all my teachers

INDEX

S. NO	NAME	PAGE NO
1	Introduction: Why Learn C?	02
2	Chapter 1: Getting Started with C	06
3	Chapter 2: Basic Syntax and Structure	14
4	Chapter 3: Operators and Expressions	22
5	Chapter 4: Control Flow - Decision Making	34
6	Chapter 5: Loops - Repeating Actions	44
7	Chapter 6: Functions - Modular Programming	54
8	Chapter 7: Arrays and Strings	66
9	Chapter 8: Pointers	76
10	Chapter 9: Memory Management	86
11	Chapter 10: File I/O	96
12	Chapter 11: Debugging and Best Practices	106
13	Chapter 12: Your First C Project	118
14	Additional Resources	138
15	Appendix	144

Introduction: Why Learn C?

- History of C programming language.
- Importance of C in modern computing.
- Applications of C: system programming, embedded systems, game development, etc.
- Overview of what the reader will learn in the book.

Introduction: Why Learn C?

History of C Programming Language: C was developed in the early 1970s by Dennis Ritchie at Bell Labs as an evolution of the B programming language. It was designed to be a simple, efficient language for system programming, particularly for writing operating systems. The language's key strengths include its portability, low-level capabilities, and ease of use, making it a foundational language in the world of computing. The development of Unix, one of the most influential operating systems, was largely done in C, cementing the language's place in computing history.

Importance of C in Modern Computing: Despite being over 40 years old, C remains one of the most important and widely-used programming languages. It forms the basis of many modern languages (such as C++, C#, and Java), and its syntax and principles influence countless other programming paradigms. C offers direct access to memory and hardware, making it indispensable for low-level programming. It's also known for its efficiency, speed, and control, which is crucial for building software that runs on resource-constrained systems.

Additionally, C is the foundation for much of modern computing, powering everything from operating systems and embedded systems to network protocols and compilers. Its influence extends far beyond its own domain, making it an essential skill for any serious software developer.

Applications of C: C's versatility has led to its widespread use in many critical areas of computing:

- **System Programming:** C is used to develop operating systems, device drivers, and system utilities due to its efficiency and ability to interact directly with hardware.
- **Embedded Systems:** C is the language of choice for programming embedded systems, which power everything from medical devices to industrial machinery, due to its low-level capabilities and performance.
- **Game Development:** Many classic and modern games, especially those requiring high performance and low-latency operations, use C or C-based engines. Games need direct hardware control and fast execution, areas where C excels.
- **Compilers & Interpreters:** C is frequently used to develop compilers for other programming languages, providing the low-level control needed to translate code efficiently.
- **Networking:** Many networking protocols and services, including TCP/IP stack implementations, are written in C, making it vital for network programming.

Overview of What the Reader Will Learn: In this book, readers will embark on a structured journey to learn the C programming language. The journey will start with foundational topics such as:

- Basic C syntax (variables, operators, data types)
- Control structures (loops, conditionals)
- Functions and modular programming
- Arrays and pointers for memory management
- Advanced topics like file handling, dynamic memory, and structures

The book emphasizes hands-on learning with exercises and practical examples, ensuring that readers not only understand the theory behind C programming but also gain real-world experience in writing and debugging C code. By the end of the book, readers will have developed a solid understanding of C and be able to apply their skills in various areas, from system programming to embedded systems and beyond.

Overall, *Code with C: The Beginner's Journey* provides a strong foundation for any programmer looking to dive into one of the most powerful and influential languages in the history of computing.

1: Getting Started with C

- **What is C?**
  - A brief introduction to programming languages.
  - C's role in programming history.
- **Setting Up Your Development Environment**
  - Installing a C compiler (GCC or Clang).
  - Setting up an Integrated Development Environment (IDE) like Code::Blocks, Visual Studio Code, or using a simple text editor and terminal.
  - Writing and running your first C program.
- **Your First C Program: "Hello, World!"**
  - Detailed explanation of the program's syntax.

WHAT EACH LINE DOES
(E.G., `#INCLUDE <STDIO.H>`, `INT MAIN()`, `PRINTF()`).

1 GETTING STARTED WITH C

What is C?

A Brief Introduction to Programming Languages:

Programming languages serve as a bridge between human instructions and machine execution. A computer can only understand binary (0s and 1s), but humans think in logical, structured commands. Programming languages provide us with a syntax to write commands in a more readable form that the computer can eventually understand and execute.

Languages can broadly be classified into:

- **Low-level languages** (such as Assembly and Machine code) provide a way to write instructions very close to the computer's hardware. They offer precise control over system resources, but they are often difficult to read, write, and debug.
- **High-level languages** (like Python, Java, and Ruby) abstract away hardware details, making it easier to write programs without worrying about memory management or machine architecture.

C occupies a unique position between high- and low-level languages. It's powerful like a low-level language, offering direct access to memory and hardware, but it also has higher-level abstractions, making it easier to manage complex tasks compared to purely low-level programming.

C's Role in Programming History:

C was created in 1972 by Dennis Ritchie at **Bell Labs** as an evolution of the B programming language. C's primary goal was to simplify the development of the **Unix operating system** while making it portable across different computer architectures. Before C, operating systems were written in assembly language, making them difficult to modify and maintain.

C's combination of **power** and **portability** made it revolutionary. Code written in C could be compiled and run on any machine with minimal changes. This was particularly important for Unix, which needed to be portable across multiple hardware platforms. Today, C remains one of the most influential programming languages and is often referred to as the "mother" of modern programming languages because many popular languages (like C++, C#, Java, and even Python) trace their syntax and concepts to C.

Key points that define C's role in history:

- **Portability**: C's design allowed programs written on one machine to be easily transferred to another machine, which was a game-changer for software development in the 1970s and beyond.
- **Efficiency**: C is known for its speed and low-level capabilities, which made it ideal for system programming, such as building operating systems, compilers, and embedded systems.
- **Influence on other languages**: C laid the foundation for many subsequent programming languages (like C++, Java, and even newer ones like Rust).

Setting Up Your Development Environment

Installing a C Compiler:

A C compiler is essential for converting the human-readable code you write into machine-readable code (binary).

It translates your C program into an executable file that the computer can run. To run C programs on your computer, you need to install a compiler.

Popular C Compilers:

- **GCC (GNU Compiler Collection)**: This is one of the most widely used open-source compilers, supporting not only C but other languages like C++, Java, and Fortran. It is available on Linux, Windows (via MinGW), and macOS.

    Installation for GCC:

    o **Linux**: Most Linux distributions come with GCC pre-installed. If not, you can install it via the terminal:

    "sudo apt-get install gcc"

- **Windows**: Download and install **MinGW** (Minimalist GNU for Windows), which provides the GCC compiler for Windows. Alternatively, you can install **Cygwin** or use **Windows Subsystem for Linux (WSL)** for a Unix-like environment.

- **macOS**: You can install GCC using the **Homebrew** package manager or by installing **Xcode Command Line Tools**:

xcode-select --install

- **Clang**: Another popular open-source compiler, often favored for its faster compilation times and better error messages. It comes pre-installed with Xcode on macOS and is available on Linux.

Setting Up an Integrated Development Environment (IDE):

An IDE is a software suite that provides a set of tools to make coding easier. It often includes:

- A code editor with syntax highlighting and autocompletion.
- A compiler to build your programs.
- A debugger to find and fix errors.
- A terminal or command-line interface for running the programs.

Some popular IDEs for C programming are:

- **Code::Blocks**: A free, open-source IDE that is simple to use and supports C/C++ programming. It comes with built-in compilers like GCC and MinGW.
- **Visual Studio Code (VS Code)**: A lightweight code editor with powerful extensions for C/C++. It supports debugging, version control, and integrates well with GCC or Clang compilers.
- **DevC++**: Another easy-to-use, free IDE for C/C++ programming with a built-in compiler (like MinGW).

Alternatively, you can use a **simple text editor** (e.g., Sublime Text, Atom, Notepad++) for writing code and **terminal/command prompt** for compiling and running the program:

- **Windows**: Install MinGW or another GCC-compatible toolchain.
- **Linux/macOS**: Open the terminal and use commands like `gcc` for compiling.

Writing and Running Your First C Program:

Now that your development environment is set up, let's write and run a basic program. Follow these steps:

1. **Open your IDE** (or text editor if using a simpler setup).
2. **Create a new file** and save it as `hello.c` (the `.c` extension is standard for C source files).
3. Type the following code into the file

```
#include <stdio.h> // Include standard input/output library
int main() { // The entry point of the program
    printf("Hello, World!\n"); // Print a message to the screen
    return 0; // Return 0 to indicate successful execution
}
```

4. **Save the file** and compile it:

- In **Code::Blocks** or **DevC++**, simply click **Build** or **Compile**.
- In the **terminal** (Linux/macOS), you can compile using

gcc hello.c -o hello

5. **Run the program**:

- On **Windows**, run it from the terminal

hello.exe

On **Linux/macOS**, you can execute it as:

./hello

When executed, the output will be:

Hello, World!

Your First C Program: "Hello, World!"
Detailed Explanation of the Program's Syntax:

1. **`#include <stdio.h>`**:
   This line is a **preprocessor directive**. In C, the `#include` directive is used to include external files into your program. Here, we are including the standard input/output library (`stdio.h`) so we can use functions like `printf()` to output text to the screen.

   The **preprocessor** runs before the compilation starts and processes these directives. `stdio.h` contains function declarations for input/output operations, such as reading data from the user or printing text to the screen.

2. **`int main()`**:
   The `main()` function is the **entry point** of every C program. When you run a C program, execution always starts from `main()`. The `int` before `main()` indicates that this function will return an integer to the operating system when the program finishes running.
   - `main()` is where your code starts executing.
   - The return value of `main()` typically tells the system whether the program finished successfully (`return 0;`) or encountered an error (any non-zero value).

3. **`{` and `}`**:
   These curly braces define the **body** of the `main()` function. Everything between the `{` and `}` is part of the `main()` function, and the program executes these statements sequentially.

4. `printf("Hello, World!\n");`:
   `printf()` is the standard function used to print output to the screen. The text inside the quotes is called a **string literal**. In this case, the string `"Hello, World!"` will be printed. The `\n` is a **newline character**, which moves the cursor to the next line after printing the message.
   - `printf` is powerful and can be used to print text, variables, or formatted data (e.g., numbers, characters, or floating-point values).
5. `return 0;`:
   This statement marks the **end** of the `main()` function. The `return 0;` indicates that the program finished successfully. In C, returning `0` from `main()` is the standard way to indicate success to the operating system.
   - Returning other values can indicate an error. For example, `return 1;` or any non-zero value might signal an abnormal program termination.

By the end of this chapter, you will have:

- Installed and set up a development environment.
- Written your first C program and understood its basic components.
- Compiled and executed your program to see the output.

As you move forward in the book, you'll dive deeper into C's features, such as variables, data types, loops, functions, and memory management. This chapter lays the foundation for understanding how C works, giving you a solid starting point to begin exploring the language's full capabilities.

2: Basic Syntax and Structure

- **Structure of a C Program**
    - Header files and libraries.
    - Main function: Entry point of a C program.
    - Semicolons, braces, and parentheses.
- **Variables and Data Types**
    - Integer types (`int`, `short`, `long`).
    - Floating-point types (`float`, `double`).
    - Characters (`char`).
    - Defining and initializing variables.
    - Type conversion and type casting.
- **Comments**
    - Single-line (`//`) and multi-line (`/* ... */`) comments.
    - The importance of commenting your code.

2. Basic Syntax and Structure

2.1 Structure of a C Program

The structure of a C program is fundamental to understanding how a C program is executed and how the various components interact with each other. A well-structured C program typically consists of the following elements:

1. **Header Files and Libraries**

    Header files and libraries provide essential functionality that is used throughout a C program. These include standard libraries for input/output operations, mathematical functions, string manipulations, and more. Header files are included at the top of the program using the `#include` directive.

    o **Standard Libraries**: Common libraries such as `stdio.h` for input and output, `stdlib.h` for memory allocation, and `math.h` for mathematical functions are often included at the beginning of most programs.

    ```
    #include <stdio.h>  // Standard input/output functions
    #include <stdlib.h> // Standard utility functions (e.g., memory management)
    #include <math.h>   // Mathematical functions (e.g., sin(), cos(), sqrt())
    ```

    o **User-defined Libraries**: In addition to standard libraries, developers can create their own header files to encapsulate commonly used functions or variables.

    ```
    #include "my_header.h"  // A custom header file
    ```

2. **The `main` Function: Entry Point of a C Program**

   The `main()` function is the entry point of any C program. When the program is executed, the operating system starts by calling the `main()` function. It is where the program's execution begins.

   - **Return Type**: The `main()` function usually returns an integer value to the operating system. A return value of 0 indicates successful execution, while non-zero values typically indicate errors or abnormal terminations.

     ```
     int main() {
         // program code
         return 0;  // return value of 0 indicates successful execution
     }
     ```

   - **Function Body**: The body of the `main()` function contains the code that will be executed when the program runs. Code within `main()` can include variable declarations, control structures, function calls, and other operations.

3. **Semicolons, Braces, and Parentheses**

   Understanding how to use semicolons, braces, and parentheses correctly is critical for writing syntactically correct C code.

   - **Semicolons (`;`)**: In C, each statement must be terminated with a semicolon. This tells the compiler that the statement has ended and that the next statement is starting.
     - Example:

       ```
       int x = 10;   // semicolon marks the end of the statement
       ```

- **Braces ({ })**: Braces are used to group related statements together. For example, they are used to define blocks of code inside functions, loops, and conditionals. Every opening brace { must have a corresponding closing brace }.
  - Example:

    ```
    if (x > 5) {
        printf("x is greater than 5");
    }
    ```

- **Parentheses (( ))**: Parentheses are used to enclose arguments in function calls, to define the conditions in `if`, `while`, `for` loops, and to group expressions.
  - Example:

    ```
    if (x > 5) {   // condition enclosed in parentheses
        // code block
    }
    ```

1.2 Variables and Data Types

In C, variables are used to store data values, and each variable must be associated with a specific data type. Understanding data types is crucial for proper memory management and for preventing errors.

1. **Integer Types** (`int`, `short`, `long`)
   - `int`: The `int` type is used to store integer values. The size of an `int` depends on the machine architecture, but it is typically 4 bytes on modern systems.

     ```
     int age = 25;
     ```

   - `short`: The `short` type is used to store smaller integer values. It is typically 2 bytes in size.

     ```
     short temperature = -5;
     ```

- **long**: The `long` type is used to store larger integer values. On many systems, it is 8 bytes in size.

    ```
    long population = 7800000000;
    ```

2. **Floating-point Types** (`float`, `double`)

    Floating-point types are used to store numbers with decimal points.

    - **float**: A `float` is used to store single-precision floating-point numbers. It typically uses 4 bytes of memory.

        ```
        float pi = 3.14;
        ```

    - **double**: A `double` is used to store double-precision floating-point numbers, offering more precision than `float`. It typically uses 8 bytes of memory.

        ```
        double gravitational_constant = 9.81;
        ```

3. **Character Type (`char`)**
    - **char**: A `char` is used to store a single character. It typically uses 1 byte of memory. Characters are enclosed in single quotes (`'`), unlike strings which are enclosed in double quotes (`"`).

        ```
        char grade = 'A';
        ```

4. **Defining and Initializing Variables**
    - A variable is declared by specifying its type followed by its name.

        ```
        int count;  // Declaration of an integer variable
        ```

- A variable can be initialized at the time of declaration:

  ```
  int count = 0;  // Declaration and initialization of the variable
  ```

5. **Type Conversion and Type Casting**
   - **Implicit Type Conversion** (Type Promotion): C automatically converts data types when necessary. For example, if you assign a `float` to an `int` variable, the fractional part will be discarded.

     ```
     float pi = 3.14;
     int x = pi;  // Implicit type conversion from float to int (x becomes 3)
     ```

   - **Explicit Type Casting**: You can manually convert a variable from one type to another using type casting.

     ```
     double pi = 3.1415926535;
     int x = (int)pi;  // Explicit type casting from double to int
     ```

1.3 Comments

Comments are essential in writing readable and maintainable code. They are not executed by the program but serve as annotations to explain the code's purpose or clarify complex logic.

1. **Single-line Comments (//)**

   Single-line comments begin with // and continue to the end of the line. They are often used for brief explanations.

   ```
   int x = 10;  // Initialize x with the value 10
   ```

2. **Multi-line Comments (/* ... */)**

   Multi-line comments are used for longer explanations or for commenting out larger sections of code. They begin with /* and end with */.

   ```
   /* This is a multi-line comment.
      It can span several lines and is useful for
   long explanations or
      temporarily disabling code during debugging.
   */
   ```

3. **The Importance of Commenting Your Code**
   - **Improved Readability**: Comments help developers and others understand what the code is doing, which is especially useful in complex logic or algorithms.
   - **Code Maintenance**: As programs evolve, comments make it easier to maintain and modify the code in the future. They also help when debugging, as developers can mark areas for investigation or potential improvements.
   - **Collaboration**: In team environments, comments help different developers understand each other's code and provide context for why certain design decisions were made.
   - **Documentation**: Comments can serve as a lightweight form of documentation, explaining key functions, parameters, and return values.

   However, it's important not to over-comment. The goal should be to write clean, understandable code with comments used to clarify the complex or non-obvious parts.

In this chapter your have learn about Understanding the **basic syntax and structure** of a C program which is the foundation upon which all other C programming concepts are built. From header files and libraries to the role of the `main()` function, every component plays a critical role in ensuring that the program executes as expected. Proper use of **variables and data types** allows for efficient data management, while **comments** make the code more understandable and maintainable. Mastering these fundamental concepts is essential for any C programmer.

3: Operators and Expressions

- **Arithmetic Operators**
    - Addition (+), subtraction (-), multiplication (*), division (/), and modulo (%).
    - Operator precedence and associativity.
- **Relational Operators**
    - Comparing values: ==, !=, <, >, <=, >=.
- **Logical Operators**
    - AND (&&), OR (||), NOT (!).
- **Assignment Operators**
    - Basic assignment (=), compound assignments (+=, -=, etc.).
- **Increment and Decrement Operators**
    - Prefix and postfix (++, --).
- **Sample Programs**
    - Write simple programs using operators (e.g., calculator, area of shapes).

3 OPERATORS AND EXPRESSIONS

In C programming, **operators** are symbols that perform operations on variables and values. These operations range from basic arithmetic to logical comparisons and memory manipulation. Understanding how operators work is crucial for writing efficient and effective programs. This chapter will cover the most commonly used operators in C, how expressions are evaluated, and how operator precedence and associativity affect the result of an expression.

3.1 Arithmetic Operators

Arithmetic operators in C are used to perform basic mathematical operations. These operators apply to numeric data types, such as `int`, `float`, `double`, and `long`.

1. Addition (+)

The addition operator adds two values together.

Example:

```
int a = 10, b = 5;
int sum = a + b;   // sum will be 15
```

This operator is also used for string concatenation when both operands are strings.

Example:

```
char str1[] = "Hello", str2[] = " World!";
printf("%s\n", str1 + str2);   // Output: Hello World!
```

2. Subtraction (-)

The subtraction operator subtracts the second operand from the first operand.

Example:

```
int a = 10, b = 4;
int difference = a - b;   // difference will be 6
```

3. Multiplication (*)

The multiplication operator multiplies two values.

Example:

```
int a = 4, b = 5;
int product = a * b;   // product will be 20
```

4. Division (/)

The division operator divides the first operand by the second. It returns the quotient.

Example:

```
int a = 20, b = 4;
int quotient = a / b;   // quotient will be 5
```

Note: When dividing integers, C performs integer division, which discards the fractional part. To avoid this, you should use `float` or `double`.

Example (float):

```
float a = 20.0, b = 3.0;
float quotient = a / b;   // quotient will be 6.66667
```

5. Modulo (%)

The modulo operator returns the remainder of a division.

Example:

```c
int a = 20, b = 3;
int remainder = a % b;   // remainder will be 2
```

This is especially useful for tasks like checking even or odd numbers:

```c
int number = 5;
if (number % 2 == 0) {
    printf("Even\n");
} else {
    printf("Odd\n");
}
```

Operator Precedence and Associativity

Operator precedence defines the order in which operations are performed in an expression. C follows specific rules to decide which operator to evaluate first in a given expression.

- **Arithmetic operators** like * (multiplication) and / (division) have higher precedence than + (addition) and - (subtraction).
- Operators with the **same precedence** (e.g., + and -, or * and /) are evaluated based on their **associativity**.

Associativity: Most operators in C, including arithmetic ones, are evaluated left-to-right (left-associative). However, assignment operators (=, +=, etc.) are evaluated right-to-left (right-associative).

Example:

```c
int result = 5 + 3 * 2;   // result will be 11 because * has higher precedence than +
```

Example of Associativity:

```
int a = 10;
a = 5 + 3 * 2;   // result will be 11
a += 5 * 2;      // result will be 21 (evaluates as a =
a + (5 * 2))
```

3.2 Relational Operators

Relational operators are used to compare two values and determine their relationship. The result of relational operations is a **boolean value**: `true` (1) or `false` (0).

1. Equal to (==)

Checks if two values are equal.

Example:

```
int a = 5, b = 5;
if (a == b) {
    printf("Equal\n");   // Output: Equal
}
```

2. Not equal to (!=)

Checks if two values are not equal.

Example:

```
int a = 5, b = 10;
if (a != b) {
    printf("Not Equal\n");   // Output: Not Equal
}
```

3. Less than (<)

Checks if the left operand is less than the right operand.

Example:

```c
int a = 5, b = 10;
if (a < b) {
    printf("a is less than b\n");   // Output: a is less than b
}
```

4. Greater than (>)

Checks if the left operand is greater than the right operand.

Example:

```c
int a = 10, b = 5;
if (a > b) {
    printf("a is greater than b\n");   // Output: a is greater than b
}
```

5. Less than or equal to (<=)

Checks if the left operand is less than or equal to the right operand.

Example:

```c
int a = 5, b = 5;
if (a <= b) {
    printf("a is less than or equal to b\n");   // Output: a is less than or equal to b
}
```

6. Greater than or equal to (>=)

Checks if the left operand is greater than or equal to the right operand.

Example:

```c
int a = 5, b = 5;
if (a >= b) {
    printf("a is greater than or equal to b\n");   // Output: a is greater than or equal to b
}
```

3.3 Logical Operators

Logical operators are used to perform logical operations, often in conditional statements. They operate on boolean values (true/false).

1. AND (&&)

The AND operator returns `true` if **both** operands are true.

Example:

```
int a = 5, b = 10;
if (a > 0 && b > 0) {
    printf("Both conditions are true\n");   // Output: Both conditions are true
}
```

2. OR (||)

The OR operator returns `true` if **at least one** operand is true.

Example:

```
int a = -5, b = 10;
if (a > 0 || b > 0) {
    printf("At least one condition is true\n");   // Output: At least one condition is true
}
```

3. NOT (!)

The NOT operator negates the boolean value of the operand. If the operand is true, it returns false, and if it is false, it returns true.

Example:

```
int a = 5;
if (!(a < 0)) {
    printf("a is not less than 0\n");   // Output: a is not less than 0
}
```

3.4 Assignment Operators

Assignment operators are used to assign values to variables. The most basic assignment operator is the single equal sign (=), but there are also **compound assignment operators** that allow you to perform an operation and assignment in one step.

1. Basic Assignment (=)

This operator is used to assign the right-hand side value to the left-hand side variable.

Example:

```
int a = 5;   // a gets the value 5
```

2. Compound Assignment Operators

These operators combine an arithmetic operation with assignment, making the code more concise.

- **Addition assignment (+=)**: Adds the right operand to the left operand and assigns the result to the left operand.

    ```
    int a = 5;
    a += 3;   // a = a + 3, so a becomes 8
    ```

- **Subtraction assignment (-=)**: Subtracts the right operand from the left operand and assigns the result to the left operand.

    ```
    int a = 5;
    a -= 3;   // a = a - 3, so a becomes 2
    ```

- **Multiplication assignment (*=)**: Multiplies the left operand by the right operand and assigns the result to the left operand.

    ```
    int a = 5;
    a *= 2;   // a = a * 2, so a becomes 10
    ```

- **Division assignment (/=)**: Divides the left operand by the right operand and assigns the result to the left operand.

    ```
    int a = 10;
    a /= 2;   // a = a / 2, so a becomes 5
    ```

- **Modulo assignment (%=)**: Takes the modulo of the left operand with the right operand and assigns the result to the left operand.

    ```
    int a = 10;
    a %= 3;   // a = a % 3, so a becomes 1
    ```

3.5 Increment and Decrement Operators

The increment (++) and decrement (--) operators are used to increase or decrease the value of a variable by 1.

1. Prefix Increment (++a)

Increments the variable before using its value.

Example:

```
int a = 5;
int result = ++a;   // a is incremented first, so result = 6, and a becomes 6
```
2. Postfix Increment (a++)

Uses the current value of the variable before incrementing it.

Example:

```
int a = 5;
int result = a++;  // result = 5 (current value of a),
and a becomes 6
```

3. Prefix Decrement (--a)

Decrements the variable before using its value.

Example:

```
int a = 5;
int result = --a;  // a is decremented first, so result
= 4, and a becomes 4
```

4. Postfix Decrement (a--)

Uses the current value of the variable before decrementing it.

Example:

```
int a = 5;
int result = a--;  // result = 5 (current value of a),
and a becomes 4
```

3.6 Sample Programs

Now, let's look at some sample programs to put all these operators into practice.

1. Calculator Program

A simple calculator that performs basic arithmetic operations.

```c
#include <stdio.h>

int main() {
    int a, b, sum, diff, product, quotient, remainder;

    printf("Enter two integers: ");
    scanf("%d %d", &a, &b);

    sum = a + b;
    diff = a - b;
    product = a * b;
    quotient = a / b;
    remainder = a % b;
    printf("Sum: %d\n", sum);
    printf("Difference: %d\n", diff);
    printf("Product: %d\n", product);
    printf("Quotient: %d\n", quotient);
    printf("Remainder: %d\n", remainder);
    return 0;
}
```

2. Area of a Circle

A program that calculates the area of a circle given its radius.

```
#include <stdio.h>
#define PI 3.14159

int main() {
    float radius, area;

    printf("Enter the radius of the circle: ");
    scanf("%f", &radius);

    area = PI * radius * radius;

    printf("Area of the circle: %.2f\n", area);

    return 0;
}
```

In this chapter we have explored the **different types of operators** used in C, including **arithmetic, relational, logical, assignment**, and **increment/decrement operators**.

Understanding how these operators work and how operator precedence and associativity affect the evaluation of expressions is fundamental to writing correct and efficient C programs. We also saw how to combine operators to perform complex operations and how to use sample programs to apply these concepts in real-world scenarios. By mastering operators, you'll be able to write more powerful and optimized C code.

4: Control Flow - Decision Making

- **If-Else Statements**
    - The basic if statement: `if`, `else`, and `else if`.
    - Nesting if statements.
    - Example: Odd or even checker.
- **Switch-Case Statements**
    - When to use `switch` over multiple `if-else`.
    - Example: Day of the week program.
- **Ternary Operator**
    - Shortcut for `if-else`: `condition ? expr1 : expr2`.

4 CONTROL FLOW - DECISION MAKING

Control flow in programming refers to the order in which individual statements or instructions are executed. Decision-making structures are a fundamental part of programming because they allow the program to make choices based on specific conditions. In C, decision-making can be done using the **if-else statements, switch-case statements**, and **ternary operator**. This chapter will cover each of these structures in detail, with practical examples.

4.1 If-Else Statements

The **if-else** statement is the most common decision-making structure in C. It evaluates a condition and, based on whether the condition is true or false, it executes one of the two blocks of code.

1. The Basic If Statement

The basic syntax for an `if` statement is:

```
if (condition) {
    // code to be executed if the condition is true
}
```

If the condition evaluates to `true` (non-zero), the block of code inside the `if` statement is executed. If the condition is `false` (zero), the code inside the `if` block is skipped.

Example:

```
int a = 10;

if (a > 0) {
    printf("a is positive\n");
}
```

In this example, since a is greater than 0, the output will be:

```
a is positive
```

2. The If-Else Statement

The `if-else` statement allows for two possible outcomes. If the condition is true, the first block of code is executed; otherwise, the code inside the `else` block is executed.

Syntax:

```
if (condition) {
    // code if condition is true
} else {
    // code if condition is false
}
```

Example:

```
int a = -5;

if (a > 0) {
    printf("a is positive\n");
} else {
    printf("a is non-positive\n");
}
```

In this example, since a is negative, the output will be:

```
a is non-positive
```

3. Else-If Ladder

When you have multiple conditions to check, you can chain multiple `if-else` statements together using `else if`. This allows you to check more than two conditions.

Syntax:

```
if (condition1) {
    // code if condition1 is true
} else if (condition2) {
    // code if condition2 is true
} else {
    // code if no condition is true
}
```

Example:

```
int a = 0;

if (a > 0) {
    printf("a is positive\n");
} else if (a < 0) {
    printf("a is negative\n");
} else {
    printf("a is zero\n");
}
```

In this example, since `a` is 0, the output will be:

```
a is zero
```

4. Nesting If Statements

You can also place one `if` statement inside another. This is called **nested if-else**. It allows you to perform more complex decision-making.

Example:

```
int a = 10, b = 20;

if (a > 0) {
    if (b > 0) {
        printf("Both a and b are positive\n");
    } else {
        printf("a is positive, but b is not\n");
    }
} else {
    printf("a is not positive\n");
}
```

Here, the first `if` checks if `a` is positive. If so, it checks whether `b` is positive. Since both conditions are true, the output will be:

```
Both a and b are positive
```

4.2 Switch-Case Statements

A `switch-case` statement provides a way to execute different parts of code based on the value of a single variable. It is a more efficient way of handling multiple `if-else` statements when you have many conditions based on the same variable.

1. Basic Syntax of Switch-Case

The syntax of a `switch` statement is as follows:

```
switch (expression) {
    case value1:
        // code to execute if expression equals value1
        break;
    case value2:
        // code to execute if expression equals value2
        break;
    // more cases...
    default:
        // code to execute if no case matches
}
```

- `expression`: This is evaluated once. It can be an integer, character, or enumerated type.
- `case`: Each `case` specifies a value that the expression will be compared against.
- `break`: The `break` statement terminates the `switch` block. Without it, the program will "fall through" to the next case (which is generally not desired).
- `default`: This block is executed if none of the `case` values match the expression.

2. Example: Day of the Week Program

The `switch` statement is ideal when you need to select one of several possible outcomes based on a single variable, such as the day of the week.

```c
#include <stdio.h>
int main() {
    int day = 3;
    switch (day) {
        case 1:
            printf("Monday\n");
            break;
        case 2:
            printf("Tuesday\n");
            break;
        case 3:
            printf("Wednesday\n");
            break;
        case 4:
            printf("Thursday\n");
            break;
        case 5:
            printf("Friday\n");
            break;
        case 6:
            printf("Saturday\n");
            break;
        case 7:
            printf("Sunday\n");
            break;
        default:
            printf("Invalid day\n");
    }

    return 0;
}
```

In this example, `day` is 3, so the output will be:

```
Wednesday
```

3. When to Use Switch Over Multiple If-Else

The `switch-case` structure is more readable and efficient than using multiple `if-else` statements when you need to compare the same expression against many possible values. The `switch` statement can also be more performant, especially if there are many `case` values, as it can use a jump table internally.

However, `switch` can only compare a single expression against constant values, which is why it is limited to discrete values (e.g., integers or characters).

4.3 Ternary Operator

The **ternary operator** is a shorthand for simple `if-else` statements. It is often used when you need to assign a value based on a condition.

Syntax of the Ternary Operator
```
condition ? expr1 : expr2;
```

- If the condition is `true`, `expr1` is evaluated and returned.
- If the condition is `false`, `expr2` is evaluated and returned.

Example:
```
int a = 5, b = 10;
int max = (a > b) ? a : b;  // If a > b, max = a; otherwise, max = b
printf("The maximum value is: %d\n", max);
```

In this example, the condition (a > b) is false, so the output will be:

```
The maximum value is: 10
```

Advantages of the Ternary Operator

- The ternary operator allows you to write more compact code for simple conditions.
- It is ideal for assignments, as it helps avoid the verbosity of a full `if-else` statement.

Example of Nested Ternary Operator: You can even nest ternary operators, though it can reduce readability if overused.

```
int a = 10, b = 20, c = 5;
int largest = (a > b) ? (a > c ? a : c) : (b > c ? b : c);
printf("The largest number is: %d\n", largest);
```

Here, the ternary operator first compares a and b, then compares the larger of those with c to determine the largest number. The output will be:

```
The largest number is: 20
```

In this chapter, we've covered the following control flow structures:

1. **If-Else Statements**: The basic structure for decision-making in C. We discussed how to use `if`, `else`, and `else if`, as well as how to nest `if` statements for more complex conditions.
2. **Switch-Case Statements**: An alternative to multiple `if-else` statements when comparing the same variable against multiple possible values. We saw an example of how to use `switch` to determine the day of the week.
3. **Ternary Operator**: A shorthand for simple `if-else` statements. It allows you to evaluate conditions and return one of two values in a single line of code.

By mastering these control structures, you can write more flexible and efficient programs that can make decisions based on user input, program state, or other dynamic conditions. Understanding when and how to use each of these control flow mechanisms is essential for writing clean, readable, and maintainable code.

5: Loops - Repeating Actions

- **For Loop**
    - Syntax: `for(initialization; condition; increment/decrement).`
    - Example: Print numbers 1 to 10.
- **While Loop**
    - Syntax: `while(condition).`
    - Example: Sum of natural numbers.
- **Do-While Loop**
    - Syntax: `do { } while(condition);.`
    - Example: Menu-driven program that continues until the user exits.
- **Breaking Out of Loops**
    - `break` and `continue` statements.

5. LOOPS - REPEATING ACTIONS

In programming, **loops** are essential tools that allow us to repeat a block of code multiple times without having to write the same code over and over again. Loops are particularly useful when performing repetitive tasks such as iterating over collections of data, processing user input, or performing calculations until a certain condition is met.

Loops typically consist of the following components:

- A **condition** to test whether the loop should continue.
- A **body** containing the code that needs to be executed.
- An **update** (such as incrementing or decrementing a counter variable) to modify the loop's condition.

Understanding how and when to use different types of loops—**for loops**, **while loops**, and **do-while loops**—is crucial for writing efficient and readable code. This chapter covers these types of loops in detail, along with special keywords like `break` and `continue` that control the flow inside loops.

1. The For Loop

The **for loop** is the most common and versatile type of loop in programming. It is particularly well-suited for scenarios where you know in advance how many times you need to repeat a specific task. It's commonly used to iterate through arrays or lists, or to execute code a specific number of times based on a known range.

Syntax:
```
for (initialization; condition; increment/decrement) {
    // Code to be executed repeatedly
}
```

- **Initialization**: This is executed once, at the beginning of the loop. It typically sets up a loop variable (like a counter).
- **Condition**: This condition is evaluated before each iteration. If it evaluates to `true`, the code inside the loop will run. If it's `false`, the loop will terminate.
- **Increment/Decrement**: After each iteration, the loop variable is modified according to this part of the syntax. This typically increases or decreases a counter.

Example: Print numbers from 1 to 10

Let's take a look at a simple example where we use a **for loop** to print the numbers 1 through 10.

```
#include <stdio.h>

int main() {
    for (int i = 1; i <= 10; i++) {
        printf("%d\n", i);  // Print the current value of i
    }
    return 0;
}
```

Here's a breakdown:

- **Initialization**: `int i = 1` sets up the loop variable `i` to 1.
- **Condition**: `i <= 10` means the loop will continue running as long as `i` is less than or equal to 10.
- **Increment**: `i++` increases the value of `i` by 1 on each iteration.

As a result, the program prints the numbers 1 through 10, one per line.

Use Case:

The **for loop** is often used when:

- You know the exact number of iterations.
- You need to iterate over an array or list.
- You want precise control over the loop variable.

2. The While Loop

The **while loop** is useful when the number of iterations is not known beforehand, and you need to repeat a block of code as long as a specific condition holds true. The condition is checked before each iteration, and if it evaluates to `false` at the start, the code inside the loop will not run at all.

Syntax:
```
while (condition) {
    // Code to be executed repeatedly
}
```

- **Condition**: This is evaluated before each iteration. If the condition is `true`, the loop runs; if `false`, the loop exits.

Example: Sum of natural numbers up to n

Here's an example that uses a **while loop** to calculate the sum of all natural numbers up to a given value n.

```c
#include <stdio.h>

int main() {
    int n, sum = 0;

    printf("Enter a number: ");
    scanf("%d", &n);

    int i = 1;
    while (i <= n) {  // Loop will continue until i exceeds n
        sum += i;      // Add i to the sum
        i++;           // Increment i by 1
    }

    printf("The sum of natural numbers up to %d is: %d\n", n, sum);
    return 0;
}
```

In this example:

- The loop continues as long as i is less than or equal to n.
- The sum of the numbers from 1 to n is accumulated in the sum variable.
- After each iteration, i is incremented by 1.

Use Case:

A **while loop** is best when:

- The number of iterations is not known in advance.
- The loop should continue until a certain condition is met, like waiting for user input or processing items in a collection.

3. The Do-While Loop

The **do-while loop** is similar to the **while loop**, but with a crucial difference: in a **do-while loop**, the condition is checked **after** the code block executes. This means that the loop will always execute at least once, even if the condition is initially false. It's useful for situations where you want to ensure that the loop's body runs at least once before the condition is evaluated.

Syntax:
```
do {
    // Code to be executed at least once
} while (condition);
```

- **Code Block**: The code inside the `do` is executed at least once.
- **Condition**: After executing the code block, the condition is checked. If the condition is `true`, the loop continues; if `false`, the loop stops.

Example: Menu-driven program

Consider this example where a program repeatedly shows a menu until the user chooses to exit:

```c
#include <stdio.h>

int main() {
    int choice;

    do {
        printf("\nMenu:\n");
        printf("1. Add Numbers\n");
        printf("2. Subtract Numbers\n");
        printf("3. Exit\n");
        printf("Enter your choice: ");
        scanf("%d", &choice);
```

```
        switch(choice) {
            case 1:
                printf("You chose to Add Numbers.\n");
                break;
            case 2:
                printf("You chose to Subtract
Numbers.\n");
                break;
            case 3:
                printf("Exiting the program.\n");
                break;
            default:
                printf("Invalid choice. Please try
again.\n");
        }
    } while (choice != 3);  // Loop continues until the
user chooses to exit (choice == 3)

    return 0;
}
```

In this example:

- The loop keeps asking the user for input until they enter 3 to exit.
- The menu is displayed, and based on the user's input, the corresponding action is taken.

Use Case:

The **do-while loop** is perfect when:

- You need to execute the loop body at least once, regardless of the condition.
- Examples include asking for user input or displaying menus where the user is prompted repeatedly until a valid input is provided.

4. Breaking Out of Loops

Sometimes, you may want to exit a loop prematurely before its condition has been met. For this, the **break** statement is used. Additionally, the **continue** statement allows you to skip the current iteration and continue with the next one.

Break Statement:

The break statement is used to exit the current loop immediately, regardless of the loop's condition. It is useful when a certain condition is met, and you no longer need to continue the loop.

Example: Breaking out of a loop when a specific condition is met

```
for (int i = 1; i <= 10; i++) {
    if (i == 5) {
        break;  // Exit the loop when i is 5
    }
    printf("%d\n", i);  // Print the current value of i
}
```

In this example:

- The loop prints the numbers 1 through 4 and exits immediately when i reaches 5 due to the break statement.

Continue Statement:

The continue statement causes the current iteration of the loop to end, and the loop proceeds with the next iteration, skipping the rest of the code for the current cycle.

Example: Skipping even numbers
```
for (int i = 1; i <= 10; i++) {
    if (i % 2 == 0) {
        continue;   // Skip the even numbers
    }
    printf("%d\n", i);   // Print the current value of i
}
```

In this case:

- The loop prints only odd numbers (1, 3, 5, 7, 9) because the continue statement skips the even numbers.

In this chapter we have explored the following concepts:

- **For Loop**: Ideal for situations where the number of iterations is known in advance. Commonly used for iterating over arrays or performing a set number of operations.
- **While Loop**: Suitable for scenarios where the number of iterations is not known, and the loop runs as long as a condition is `true`.
- **Do-While Loop**: Ensures that the loop's body executes at least once, making it useful for menu-driven programs or repeated user input prompts.
- **Break and Continue**: Control statements like `break` and `continue` provide finer control over loop execution, allowing for early termination or skipping of certain iterations.

By mastering these types of loops and understanding their respective use cases, you can write more efficient, clean, and flexible code to handle repetitive tasks in your programs.

6: Functions - Modular Programming

- **What is a Function?**
    - The role of functions in C.
    - Function definition, declaration, and call.
    - Example: A function to calculate the area of a circle.
- **Function Arguments and Return Types**
    - Passing data to functions (parameters).
    - Returning values from functions (`int`, `float`, etc.).
    - Example: A function that swaps two numbers.
- **Recursion**

Simple recursion explained (e.g., factorial function).

6 FUNCTIONS - MODULAR PROGRAMMING

In software development, organizing code into manageable, reusable chunks is critical for writing clean, maintainable, and efficient programs. One of the most powerful tools for achieving modularity is the **function**. Functions allow you to break down complex problems into smaller, more manageable tasks, which makes your code easier to write, debug, and maintain.

In this chapter, we will explore **functions** in C programming. We will cover the basics of defining and using functions, how to pass data to them via parameters, how to return values, and introduce the concept of **recursion**.

1. What is a Function?

A **function** in C is a block of code that performs a specific task and can be invoked by other parts of the program whenever needed. Functions allow you to:

- **Encapsulate logic**: Group a set of related statements into a single unit.
- **Reuse code**: Once defined, a function can be called any number of times, reducing redundancy.
- **Improve maintainability**: Changes to the function's logic only need to be made in one place.
- **Enhance readability**: By breaking down a complex task into smaller functions, your code becomes more readable and easier to understand.

The Role of Functions in C:

Functions play several important roles in a C program:

- **Code Reusability**: Functions allow you to reuse the same code multiple times, which helps reduce redundancy and minimize errors.
- **Modularity**: Functions break a program into smaller, logically distinct blocks. This modularity enhances readability and makes the program easier to maintain.
- **Testing and Debugging**: Since functions are self-contained, they can be tested independently. This modular approach helps isolate issues and makes debugging easier.
- **Abstraction**: Functions allow you to hide complex logic behind simple function calls, which means that you don't need to understand the internal workings of a function to use it effectively.

Components of a Function:

To use functions in C, there are three important concepts:

1. **Function Definition**: The body of the function, where the task is performed.
2. **Function Declaration (Prototype)**: A declaration that informs the compiler about the function's name, return type, and the types of arguments it takes.
3. **Function Call**: The point where the function is invoked in the program.

2. Function Definition, Declaration, and Call

Understanding how to define, declare, and call functions is fundamental to programming in C.

Function Declaration:

A function **declaration** or **prototype** specifies the function's signature: its return type, name, and the types of its parameters (if any). The function declaration is typically placed at the beginning of the program or before the function call in the `main()` function.

Syntax:

```
return_type function_name(parameter1_type parameter1_name, parameter2_type parameter2_name, ...);
```

- **return_type**: The type of value the function returns (e.g., `int`, `float`, `void`).
- **function_name**: The name you use to refer to the function.
- **parameters**: Variables passed to the function that provide it with the data it needs to operate.

Example:

```
float calculate_area(float radius);
```

This declares a function `calculate_area` that takes a `float` argument (`radius`) and returns a `float` value (the area of the circle).

Function Definition:

The **function definition** includes both the declaration and the actual code that performs the function's task. This is where the function's logic is implemented.

Syntax:

```
return_type function_name(parameter1_type parameter1_name, parameter2_type parameter2_name, ...)
{
    // Function body: code to perform the task
}
```

Example:

```
float calculate_area(float radius) {
    return 3.14159 * radius * radius;   // Formula for area of a circle
}
```

Function Call:

The **function call** is where you invoke a function in your program, passing appropriate arguments to it.

Syntax:

```
function_name(argument1, argument2, ...);
```

Example:

```
float area = calculate_area(5.0);   // Calling the function with radius = 5.0
```

3. Function Arguments and Return Types

Functions can accept data through **parameters** and return results using the `return` statement. These two aspects—**passing data to functions** and **returning values**—are fundamental for making functions more flexible and functional.

Passing Data to Functions (Parameters)

Parameters are used to pass information into a function. They act as placeholders for the values you provide when calling the function. C supports two main ways to pass parameters:

1. **Pass-by-value**: A copy of the argument is passed to the function. The function operates on the copy, and any changes made inside the function do not affect the original value.
2. **Pass-by-reference** (using pointers): The address (reference) of the argument is passed to the function, which allows the function to modify the actual value of the argument.

Returning Values from Functions

A function can return a value using the `return` keyword. The type of the returned value must match the function's return type. For example, a function that calculates the area of a circle should return a `float` value if the area is a decimal number.

If a function does not need to return any value, its return type should be `void`.

Example: A function that swaps two numbers

Here's an example of a function that swaps two integers using **pass-by-reference**:

```c
#include <stdio.h>

// Function Declaration
void swap(int *a, int *b);

int main() {
    int x = 10, y = 20;
    printf("Before swapping: x = %d, y = %d\n", x, y);

    // Function Call
    swap(&x, &y);   // Passing the addresses of x and y

    printf("After swapping: x = %d, y = %d\n", x, y);
    return 0;
}

// Function Definition
void swap(int *a, int *b) {
    int temp = *a;  // Dereferencing to get the value of a
    *a = *b;        // Dereferencing to assign the value of b to a
    *b = temp;      // Assigning the temporary value to b
}
```

Explanation:

- In the `swap` function, the arguments are pointers (`int *a, int *b`), so the function can directly modify the values of `x` and `y` in the `main()` function.
- The `&` operator is used in the function call to pass the addresses of `x` and `y`.
- The function swaps the values by dereferencing the pointers (`*a, *b`).

This technique is called **pass-by-reference** because we're passing the memory addresses (pointers) of the variables rather than their copies.

4. Recursion

Recursion is a programming technique where a function calls itself to solve smaller subproblems. Recursion is often used when a problem can be broken down into simpler, smaller instances of the same problem. Recursion requires a **base case** to prevent infinite recursion.

How Recursion Works:

A recursive function typically has two parts:

1. **Base Case**: A simple condition that stops the recursion. If the base case is met, the function returns a value without calling itself.
2. **Recursive Case**: The part of the function that calls itself, typically with a smaller or simpler input.

Example: Factorial Function

The factorial of a number n (denoted as n!) is defined as:

- n! = n * (n-1)! for n > 0
- 0! = 1 (base case)

Here's how we can implement a recursive function to calculate the factorial of a number:

```c
#include <stdio.h>

// Function Declaration
int factorial(int n);

int main() {
    int num = 5;
    printf("Factorial of %d is: %d\n", num, factorial(num));
    return 0;
}

// Function Definition
int factorial(int n) {
    if (n == 0) {  // Base case: factorial of 0 is 1
        return 1;
    } else {
        return n * factorial(n - 1);  // Recursive call
    }
}
```

Explanation:

- The `factorial` function calls itself with the argument `n-1` until it reaches the base case (`n == 0`), where it returns 1.
- Each recursive call multiplies the current `n` by the result of `factorial(n - 1)`, effectively building the factorial from the bottom up.

For `factorial(5)`, the calls will unfold like this:

- `factorial(5)` returns 5 * `factorial(4)`
- `factorial(4)` returns 4 * `factorial(3)`
- `factorial(3)` returns 3 * `factorial(2)`
- `factorial(2)` returns 2 * `factorial(1)`
- `factorial(1)` returns 1 * `factorial(0)`
- `factorial(0)` returns 1 (base case)
- The values are then multiplied as the recursive calls unwind.

This results in:

`factorial(5) = 5 * 4 * 3 * 2 * 1 = 120`

Use Cases for Recursion:

- **Mathematical computations**: Factorials, Fibonacci numbers, etc.
- **Tree traversal**: Recursion is often used in algorithms that traverse hierarchical structures like trees or graphs.
- **Divide-and-conquer algorithms**: Recursion is the backbone of algorithms like quicksort and mergesort, which divide the problem into smaller subproblems and solve them recursively.

In this chapter, we've explored the concept of functions in C, which are key to writing modular, reusable, and maintainable code. We covered:

- **Function Definition, Declaration, and Call**: Understanding how to define, declare, and invoke functions.
- **Function Arguments and Return Types**: How to pass data to functions using parameters and return results using the `return` statement.
- **Recursion**: A powerful technique where a function calls itself to solve problems by breaking them into smaller instances of the same problem.

Mastering functions will greatly improve the structure, clarity, and efficiency of your C programs, and understanding recursion will provide you with a tool for solving complex problems in a simple and elegant manner.

7: Arrays and Strings

- **Arrays**
    - Declaring and initializing arrays.
    - Accessing array elements.
    - Example: Storing and printing a list of numbers.
- **Multi-Dimensional Arrays**
    - 2D arrays (e.g., matrix operations).
- **Strings**
    - C strings are arrays of characters.
    - Functions to manipulate strings: `strlen()`, `strcpy()`, `strcmp()`.
    - Example: Reversing a string.

7 ARRAYS AND STRINGS

In this chapter, we will explore two fundamental data structures in C: **Arrays** and **Strings**. Arrays allow us to store multiple values of the same type efficiently, while strings in C are simply arrays of characters. We will cover how to declare and manipulate arrays, how to handle multi-dimensional arrays, and how to work with strings in C.

Arrays

Arrays are collections of elements of the same type, stored in contiguous memory locations. Understanding arrays is crucial because they allow you to store and process large amounts of related data efficiently. Arrays are especially useful when you need to perform repetitive tasks on multiple pieces of data.

Declaring and Initializing Arrays

To declare an array in C, you specify the type of its elements, the array name, and the number of elements it will hold.

For example:

```
int numbers[5];   // Declares an integer array with 5 elements
```

This declares an array `numbers` that can hold 5 integers. However, it is important to note that these elements are initially uninitialized, meaning they may contain garbage values unless explicitly initialized.

To initialize an array at the time of declaration, you can provide a comma-separated list of values:

```c
int numbers[5] = {1, 2, 3, 4, 5};  // Initializes the array with specific values
```

If you do not provide all the values, the remaining elements are automatically initialized to zero:

```c
int numbers[5] = {1, 2};  // Array becomes {1, 2, 0, 0, 0}
```

You can also omit the size when initializing the array, and the compiler will automatically determine the size based on the number of elements:

```c
int numbers[] = {1, 2, 3, 4, 5};  // Size is inferred to be 5
```

Accessing Array Elements

Each element in an array is accessed using its index, starting from `0`. So, for an array of size `n`, the indices range from `0` to `n-1`.

For example, to access the first element of the array `numbers`:

```c
int firstElement = numbers[0];  // Accesses the first element
```

You can also modify array elements by referencing their indices:

```c
numbers[2] = 10;  // Changes the value of the third element to 10
```

Example: Storing and Printing a List of Numbers

Let's demonstrate a simple example where we store a list of numbers in an array and print them:

```c
#include <stdio.h>

int main() {
    // Declare and initialize an array of integers
    int numbers[5] = {1, 2, 3, 4, 5};

    // Print each element of the array using a loop
    for (int i = 0; i < 5; i++) {
        printf("%d ", numbers[i]);   // Prints each number followed by a space
    }

    return 0;
}
```

Output:

```
1 2 3 4 5
```

This program demonstrates how to store values in an array and print them using a loop.

Multi-Dimensional Arrays

While one-dimensional arrays allow you to store a list of elements, **multi-dimensional arrays** let you store data in a grid-like structure. A two-dimensional array (2D array) is essentially an array of arrays, and is often used to represent matrices or tables.

2D Arrays (Matrix Operations)

A 2D array is declared by specifying two dimensions: the number of rows and the number of columns. For example, a 3x3 matrix can be represented as:

```c
int matrix[3][3];   // A 3x3 matrix
```

This array can hold 9 elements in total, arranged in 3 rows and 3 columns.

Initialization of 2D Arrays

To initialize a 2D array, you use nested curly braces, with each set representing a row:

```c
int matrix[3][3] = {
    {1, 2, 3},
    {4, 5, 6},
    {7, 8, 9}
};
```

This initializes a 3x3 matrix with specific values. Each inner set of curly braces represents a row, and the numbers inside represent the elements in that row.

Accessing Elements in 2D Arrays

To access an element in a 2D array, you need to specify both the row and the column indices:

```c
int value = matrix[1][2];  // Accesses the element at row 1, column 2 (value is 6)
```

Example: Matrix Addition

Let's look at an example of adding two 2D matrices:

```c
#include <stdio.h>

int main() {
    // Declare and initialize two 2D matrices
    int matrix1[2][2] = {{1, 2}, {3, 4}};
    int matrix2[2][2] = {{5, 6}, {7, 8}};

    // Declare a result matrix to store the sum
    int result[2][2];
```

```c
    // Add the corresponding elements of matrix1 and matrix2
    for (int i = 0; i < 2; i++) {
        for (int j = 0; j < 2; j++) {
            result[i][j] = matrix1[i][j] + matrix2[i][j];
        }
    }

    // Print the result matrix
    for (int i = 0; i < 2; i++) {
        for (int j = 0; j < 2; j++) {
            printf("%d ", result[i][j]);  // Prints each element of the result matrix
        }
        printf("\n");
    }

    return 0;
}
```

Output:

6 8
10 12

In this example, we added two 2x2 matrices and stored the result in a third matrix, printing the sum.

Strings

In C, **strings** are simply arrays of characters terminated by a special character called the **null terminator ('\0')**. A string in C is a sequence of characters that are stored in a contiguous block of memory.

C Strings as Arrays of Characters

To declare a string, you use an array of `char` type. For example:

```c
char str[] = "Hello, world!";  // Declares and initializes a string
```

Internally, this string is represented as an array of characters, with each character stored sequentially in memory, followed by the null terminator `'\0'`.

Manipulating Strings with Functions

C provides several standard functions to manipulate strings, which are defined in the `string.h` library.

- **`strlen()`**: This function returns the length of a string, not counting the null terminator.

    ```c
    #include <stdio.h>
    #include <string.h>

    int main() {
        char str[] = "Hello";
        printf("Length of the string: %lu\n", strlen(str));  // Output: 5
        return 0;
    }
    ```

- **`strcpy()`**: This function copies one string into another.

    ```c
    char src[] = "Hello";
    char dest[10];
    strcpy(dest, src);  // Copies the string from src to dest
    printf("%s\n", dest);  // Output: Hello
    ```

- **strcmp()**: This function compares two strings lexicographically. It returns 0 if the strings are identical, a negative number if the first string is lexicographically smaller, and a positive number if it is larger.

```c
char str1[] = "apple";
char str2[] = "banana";
int result = strcmp(str1, str2);   // Compares "apple" with "banana"

if (result == 0) {
    printf("Strings are equal.\n");
} else if (result < 0) {
    printf("str1 is less than str2.\n");
} else {
    printf("str1 is greater than str2.\n");
}
```

Example: Reversing a String

Here's an example of how to reverse a string in C:

```c
#include <stdio.h>
#include <string.h>

void reverseString(char str[]) {
    int start = 0;
    int end = strlen(str) - 1;

    while (start < end) {
        // Swap the characters at positions 'start' and 'end'
        char temp = str[start];
        str[start] = str[end];
        str[end] = temp;

        start++;
        end--;
    }
}

int main() {
    char str[] = "Hello, world!";
    printf("Original string: %s\n", str);

    reverseString(str);
    printf("Reversed string: %s\n", str);

    return 0;
}
```

Output:

```
Original string: Hello, world!
Reversed string: !dlrow ,olleH
```

In this example, the `reverseString()` function swaps characters from the ends of the string towards the center, effectively reversing it.

In this chapter, we learned about the following concepts:

- **Arrays**: How to declare, initialize, and access one-dimensional arrays in C.
- **Multi-Dimensional Arrays**: Working with 2D arrays, including matrix operations such as matrix addition.
- **Strings**: Understanding strings as arrays of characters and using functions like `strlen()`, `strcpy()`, and `strcmp()` to manipulate them.

These topics are foundational in C programming and provide the tools to manage and manipulate data efficiently. Mastering arrays and strings is essential for writing effective programs, especially when dealing with large datasets or textual data.

8: Pointers

- **Introduction to Pointers**
    - What are pointers? Understanding memory addresses.
    - Declaring and initializing pointers.
    - Using the & (address-of) and * (dereferencing) operators.
- **Pointer Arithmetic**
    - Accessing elements in arrays using pointers.
    - Example: Swapping two values using pointers.
- **Pointers and Functions**
    - Passing arguments by reference to functions using pointers.

Example: Function to find the maximum of two numbers.

8 POINTERS

Introduction to Pointers
What are Pointers? Understanding Memory Addresses

In C, everything that is stored in a computer's memory has a specific location, known as its **memory address**. When you declare a variable, it is allocated a space in memory. This memory address is where the variable's value is stored. A **pointer** is simply a variable that stores the memory address of another variable. Rather than holding a value directly (like an integer, character, etc.), a pointer holds the address where the value is located.

Let's clarify this with an example:

```
int x = 10;       // Declare an integer variable 'x' and initialize it to 10
int *ptr = &x;    // Declare a pointer 'ptr' and initialize it to the address of 'x'
```

Here's what's happening:

- `x` is an integer variable with a value of `10`. Suppose it's stored at memory address `0x7fffdba0` (this is just an example; the actual memory address varies each time the program runs).
- `&x` is the **address-of operator**, which gives us the memory address where `x` is stored.
- `ptr` is a pointer variable, and it stores the memory address of `x`.

To access the value stored at the address that `ptr` is pointing to, we use the **dereferencing operator (*)**.

```
printf("%d\n", *ptr);   // Dereference the pointer 'ptr'
to get the value of 'x', which is 10
```

In this case, `*ptr` will output `10` because `ptr` points to x, which holds the value `10`.

Declaring and Initializing Pointers

A pointer is declared using the asterisk (*) symbol, which indicates that the variable will store the memory address of a specific data type. For example:

```
int *ptr;  // Declare a pointer 'ptr' that will point
to an integer
```

You can initialize the pointer when declaring it by assigning it the address of a variable:

```
int x = 10;
int *ptr = &x;  // 'ptr' now points to the address of
'x'
```

If a pointer is declared but not initialized, it may hold a garbage value, which can lead to undefined behavior if used. Therefore, it's best practice to initialize pointers to `NULL` or a valid memory address:

```
int *ptr = NULL;   // Safe initialization
```

NULL pointers are often used as a sentinel value, indicating that the pointer is not pointing to any valid memory location.

Using the & (Address-of) and * (Dereferencing) Operators

- **Address-of operator (&)**: When applied to a variable, it returns the memory address of that variable.

    ```
    int x = 10;
    int *ptr = &x;   // '&x' returns the memory
    address of 'x'
    ```

- **Dereferencing operator (*)**: When applied to a pointer, it gives the value stored at the address the pointer is pointing to.

    ```
    int x = 10;
    int *ptr = &x;
    printf("%d\n", *ptr);   // Dereference 'ptr' to
    print the value of 'x', which is 10
    ```

These two operators (& and *) are fundamental when working with pointers in C. The & operator allows you to find the address of a variable, while the * operator allows you to access the value stored at that address.

Pointer Arithmetic

Pointer arithmetic is an essential concept in C. Since a pointer holds a memory address, you can perform arithmetic operations on it to navigate through memory.

Accessing Elements in Arrays Using Pointers

Arrays in C are closely tied to pointers. The name of an array is actually a pointer to its first element. When you use an array, C treats the name of the array as a pointer to the first element.

For example, consider the following array:

```c
int arr[] = {10, 20, 30, 40, 50};
```

The array `arr` can be thought of as a pointer to the first element. To access the elements of the array using pointers, we can perform pointer arithmetic. For instance, if you want to access the second element of the array, you can increment the pointer.

```c
#include <stdio.h>

int main() {
    int arr[] = {10, 20, 30, 40, 50};
    int *ptr = arr;  // Pointer to the first element of the array

    // Access elements using pointer arithmetic
    for (int i = 0; i < 5; i++) {
        printf("%d ", *ptr);  // Dereference the pointer to get the value at that address
        ptr++;  // Move the pointer to the next element
    }
    printf("\n");

    return 0;
}
```

Explanation:

- `ptr` initially points to the first element of the array `arr[0]`.
- In the loop, we dereference `*ptr` to print the value stored at the memory address `ptr` is pointing to.
- After printing, we increment the pointer (`ptr++`), which moves the pointer to the next element in the array.

Output:

```
10 20 30 40 50
```

This shows how pointer arithmetic (`ptr++`) can be used to access the subsequent elements of an array.

Pointer Arithmetic with Different Data Types

Pointer arithmetic takes into account the size of the data type the pointer is pointing to. For example, if you have a pointer to `int`, incrementing the pointer will move it by the size of an `int` (typically 4 bytes on most systems). If the pointer is of type `char`, it will move by the size of a `char` (usually 1 byte).

```
char arr[] = {'a', 'b', 'c'};
char *ptr = arr;

ptr++;  // Moves the pointer to the next character
(moves by 1 byte)
```

On the other hand:

```
int arr[] = {1, 2, 3};
int *ptr = arr;

ptr++;  // Moves the pointer to the next integer (moves
by 4 bytes on most systems)
```

This distinction is important when performing pointer arithmetic with different types.

Pointers and Functions

Pointers are essential when passing large amounts of data to functions efficiently. In C, when you pass an argument to a function, it is passed **by value** by default, meaning the function gets a copy of the argument. However, if you want the function to modify the original variable, you can pass the **address** of the variable (i.e., a pointer), which allows the function to directly modify the data at that memory location.

Passing Arguments by Reference

When you pass a pointer to a function, the function can use it to directly modify the original variable that the pointer refers to. This is called **pass-by-reference**.

For example, let's modify the `findMax` function to find the maximum of two numbers and update the values accordingly:

```c
#include <stdio.h>

void findMax(int *a, int *b) {
    if (*a > *b) {
        *b = *a;  // Set the value of 'b' to the value of 'a'
    } else {
        *a = *b;  // Set the value of 'a' to the value of 'b'
    }
}

int main() {
    int x = 5, y = 10;
    printf("Before function call: x = %d, y = %d\n", x, y);

    findMax(&x, &y);  // Pass the addresses of 'x' and 'y' to the function

    printf("After function call: x = %d, y = %d\n", x, y);

    return 0;
}
```

Explanation:

- The function `findMax()` takes pointers to `int` as arguments, allowing it to modify the original values of `x` and `y`.
- Inside the function, we dereference the pointers to compare and update the values of `x` and `y`.

Output:

```
Before function call: x = 5, y = 10
After function call: x = 10, y = 10
```

This example demonstrates how pointers allow the function to modify the actual variables passed to it, rather than working with copies of the variables.

Passing Arrays to Functions

Arrays in C are always passed to functions as pointers, meaning when you pass an array to a function, you're passing the memory address of the first element. This is another example of pass-by-reference, and it allows the function to access and modify the array.

```
#include <stdio.h>

void printArray(int *arr, int size) {
    for (int i = 0; i < size; i++) {
        printf("%d ", arr[i]);   // Dereference the pointer to access array elements
    }
    printf("\n");
}

int main() {
    int arr[] = {1, 2, 3, 4, 5};
    printArray(arr, 5);   // Pass the array to the function

    return 0;
}
```

Explanation:

- The array `arr` is passed to the function `printArray()` as a pointer. Inside the function, the pointer is used to access the elements of the array.

Output:

1 2 3 4 5

Pointers are one of the most powerful features of the C programming language, allowing you to:

- Directly manipulate memory and data.
- Perform pointer arithmetic for tasks like iterating over arrays.
- Pass large structures like arrays and dynamically allocated memory efficiently to functions.
- Enable **pass-by-reference** to allow functions to modify variables.

Through the concepts and examples provided in this chapter, we've learned how to:

1. **Declare and initialize pointers**.
2. **Access values via pointers** using the & and * operators.
3. Use **pointer arithmetic** to navigate arrays and other data structures.
4. **Pass arguments by reference** to functions, allowing direct modification of data.

Mastering pointers is essential to understanding how memory works in C and will help you write more efficient, flexible, and powerful programs.

9: Memory Management

- **Dynamic Memory Allocation**
    - `malloc()`, `calloc()`, and `free()`.
    - Example: Allocating memory for an array during runtime.
- **Memory Leaks and Best Practices**
    - Importance of freeing memory and avoiding memory leaks.

9 MEMORY MANAGEMENT

Memory management is one of the cornerstones of efficient programming, particularly in lower-level languages such as **C** and **C++**, where developers are responsible for explicitly allocating and freeing memory. Understanding how to properly allocate, use, and free memory can make the difference between efficient, robust software and slow, buggy applications. This chapter will explore **dynamic memory allocation** techniques in C, discuss common pitfalls like **memory leaks**, and provide best practices to help you manage memory efficiently.

1. Dynamic Memory Allocation in C

In C, dynamic memory allocation allows programs to request memory at runtime based on user input or other runtime factors. This flexibility enables programs to work with large amounts of data or data structures whose size is not known at compile time.

Why Dynamic Memory Allocation?

Dynamic memory allocation is crucial when you:

- Do not know the size of your data structures at compile time (e.g., when reading data from a file).
- Need to manage memory efficiently based on the system's current memory state.
- Wish to allocate and deallocate memory as needed to minimize memory usage.

In C, the primary functions for dynamic memory allocation are `malloc()`, `calloc()`, and `realloc()`. Once the memory is allocated, it's the programmer's responsibility to release it with `free()` when it is no longer needed.

1.1 `malloc()` – Memory Allocation

The `malloc()` function (memory allocation) allocates a specified amount of memory in bytes and returns a pointer to the allocated memory. However, the contents of the memory are not initialized, meaning they can contain random data.

Syntax:

```
void *malloc(size_t size);
```

- `size`: The number of bytes to allocate.
- Returns: A pointer to the allocated memory block (of type `void*`) or `NULL` if memory allocation fails.

Example:

```c
#include <stdio.h>
#include <stdlib.h>

int main() {
    int *arr;
    int n = 5;

    // Allocate memory for an array of 5 integers
    arr = (int *)malloc(n * sizeof(int));

    if (arr == NULL) {
        printf("Memory allocation failed\n");
        return 1;
    }

    // Initialize the array elements
    for (int i = 0; i < n; i++) {
        arr[i] = i * 2;
    }
```

```
    // Output the values in the array
    for (int i = 0; i < n; i++) {
        printf("%d ", arr[i]);
    }

    // Free the allocated memory
    free(arr);
    return 0;
}
```

- **Explanation**:
    - We allocate memory for an array of 5 integers using `malloc()`.
    - After checking if the allocation was successful, we assign values to the array and print them.
    - Finally, we use `free()` to release the memory after use.

Important Notes:

- If the allocation fails (e.g., due to insufficient memory), `malloc()` returns `NULL`. Always check the return value to ensure successful memory allocation.
- **Uninitialized memory**: Since `malloc()` does not initialize the allocated memory, the values in the allocated memory are undefined (i.e., they contain garbage values).

1.2 calloc() – Contiguous Allocation

`calloc()` (contiguous allocation) works similarly to `malloc()`, but it differs in that it initializes the allocated memory to zero. This can be especially useful when you want all elements of a newly allocated array or structure to start with a known value (usually zero).

Syntax:

```
void *calloc(size_t num, size_t size);
```

- num: The number of elements.
- size: The size of each element in bytes.
- Returns: A pointer to the allocated memory block (of type `void*`) or NULL if memory allocation fails.

Example:

```c
#include <stdio.h>
#include <stdlib.h>

int main() {
    int *arr;
    int n = 5;

    // Allocate memory for an array of 5 integers and initialize to 0
    arr = (int *)calloc(n, sizeof(int));

    if (arr == NULL) {
        printf("Memory allocation failed\n");
        return 1;
    }

    // Output the array values (all should be 0)
    for (int i = 0; i < n; i++) {
        printf("%d ", arr[i]);    // Should print: 0 0 0 0 0
    }

    // Free the allocated memory
    free(arr);
    return 0;
}
```

- **Explanation**:
    - Here, `calloc()` allocates memory for an array of 5 integers, but also initializes the memory to zero.
    - The values printed are all 0, indicating that the memory was correctly initialized.

Benefits of `calloc()`:

- **Initialization**: It's often safer to use `calloc()` over `malloc()` when initializing arrays or structures because you avoid dealing with uninitialized memory.
- **Common use cases**: `calloc()` is commonly used when allocating space for large arrays or structures where a zero initialization is desired.

1.3 `free()` — Deallocating Memory

Once dynamically allocated memory is no longer needed, it must be deallocated using the `free()` function. Failing to deallocate memory leads to memory leaks, where memory that is no longer in use is still being held by the program, potentially leading to system instability and poor performance.

Syntax:

```
void free(void *ptr);
```

- `ptr`: A pointer to the memory block that should be freed.

Important Notes:

- After calling `free()`, the memory block is no longer valid, and dereferencing the pointer can lead to undefined behavior.
- It's a good practice to set the pointer to `NULL` after calling `free()` to prevent accidental access to the freed memory.

Example:

```c
#include <stdio.h>
#include <stdlib.h>

int main() {
    int *arr;
    int n = 5;

    arr = (int *)malloc(n * sizeof(int));

    if (arr == NULL) {
        printf("Memory allocation failed\n");
        return 1;
    }

    // Use the memory
    for (int i = 0; i < n; i++) {
        arr[i] = i * 2;
    }

    // Free the memory and set the pointer to NULL
    free(arr);
    arr = NULL;   // Avoid dangling pointer

    return 0;
}
```

2. Memory Leaks and Their Impact

A **memory leak** occurs when a program allocates memory dynamically but fails to release it after use. Over time, these leaks can accumulate, leading to excessive memory consumption, slowdowns, or even crashes.

Common Causes of Memory Leaks

- **Failure to call `free()`** after using dynamically allocated memory.
- **Losing references to allocated memory**: If you overwrite a pointer to dynamically allocated memory without first freeing it, you lose the ability to deallocate that memory. This results in a leak.
- **Memory allocation in a loop**: If memory is repeatedly allocated inside a loop without corresponding calls to `free()`, this can quickly result in a memory leak.

Detecting Memory Leaks

- **Manual Tracking**: One way to avoid memory leaks is to track each allocation manually by ensuring that each `malloc()`/`calloc()` call is paired with a corresponding `free()` call.
- **Tools**: Use tools like **Valgrind** or **AddressSanitizer** to detect memory leaks in C programs.

3. Best Practices for Memory Management

To write efficient and reliable code, consider the following best practices when dealing with dynamic memory allocation:

3.1 Always Check Allocation Success

- **Why?** If memory allocation fails, the returned pointer is `NULL`. If you attempt to use a `NULL` pointer, your program will crash.

Example:

```
int *arr = (int *)malloc(n * sizeof(int));
if (arr == NULL) {
    fprintf(stderr, "Memory allocation failed!\n");
    exit(1);   // Handle the error appropriately
}
```

3.2 Free Memory When It's No Longer Needed

- Always free memory when it's no longer needed to prevent memory leaks.
- Use `free()` only on memory that was allocated dynamically using `malloc()`, `calloc()`, or `realloc()`.

3.3 Avoid Double-Free Errors

- After calling `free()`, set the pointer to `NULL` to avoid accidentally freeing the same memory twice.

Example:

```
free(arr);
arr = NULL;   // Safeguard against double-free errors
```

3.4 Handle Memory Allocation Failures Gracefully

- Always ensure your program handles memory allocation failures without crashing or behaving unpredictably.
- Consider logging the failure and safely exiting or attempting to allocate less memory.

3.5 Use `realloc()` for Resizing Memory

- **`realloc()`** is used to resize a previously allocated block of memory.

Syntax:

```
void *realloc(void *ptr, size_t size);
```

- `ptr`: A pointer to the previously allocated memory.
- `size`: The new size in bytes.
- **Returns**: A new pointer to the resized memory block or `NULL` if the allocation fails.

Dynamic memory management is a fundamental aspect of efficient programming, particularly in languages like C where you must manage memory manually. By understanding how to use functions like `malloc()`, `calloc()`, and `free()`, and adhering to best practices such as checking for allocation failure, freeing memory when it's no longer needed, and avoiding memory leaks, you can ensure that your programs are both efficient and reliable.

By mastering dynamic memory allocation and deallocation, you gain control over your program's resource usage, which is especially important when working with large datasets or performance-critical applications. However, memory management mistakes such as memory leaks, dangling pointers, and double frees can lead to difficult-to-debug issues, so careful tracking and testing are essential for writing robust and efficient code.

10: File I/O

- **Introduction to File Handling**
  - Opening and closing files with `fopen()` and `fclose()`.
  - Reading from and writing to files using `fscanf()`, `fprintf()`, `fread()`, and `fwrite()`.
  - Example: Reading from a text file and displaying its contents.
- **Error Handling in File I/O**
  - Checking for file errors (e.g., file not found).

10 FILE I/O

In C programming, file handling is essential for working with data that needs to persist beyond the program's runtime. Whether you're building an application that logs information, stores user input, or manipulates large datasets, file input/output (I/O) allows you to read from and write to files. C provides functions like `fopen()`, `fclose()`, `fscanf()`, `fprintf()`, `fread()`, and `fwrite()` to manage file operations, making it a powerful tool for data management.

This chapter will cover the fundamental concepts of file I/O in C, including opening and closing files, reading from and writing to files, error handling, and binary file operations. We will also discuss the best practices to ensure efficient and safe file handling.

1. Introduction to File Handling in C

File handling in C involves interacting with files on the system's storage. To perform operations like reading, writing, or modifying files, C uses the concept of **file streams**. A file stream provides an interface between your program and the operating system's file system, allowing your program to perform file operations.

There are two main types of file handling in C:

1. **Text files** – Files that contain human-readable data (e.g., `.txt` files).
2. **Binary files** – Files that contain data in binary format (e.g., `.dat` or `.bin` files).

The **Standard Library** in C provides a rich set of file manipulation functions that can handle both text and binary files efficiently.

1.1 Opening and Closing Files: `fopen()` *and* `fclose()`

Before you can perform any operations on a file, you need to open it using the `fopen()` function, which returns a **file pointer** (`FILE *`). This pointer is then used in subsequent file operations. After you're done with the file, you must close it using `fclose()` to release system resources associated with the file.

Opening a File with `fopen()`

The `fopen()` function is used to open a file. It takes two parameters:

- **filename**: The name of the file you wish to open.
- **mode**: The access mode that specifies how the file will be used (reading, writing, appending, etc.).

Syntax:

```
FILE *fopen(const char *filename, const char *mode);
```

File Modes:

- **r**: Open for reading. The file must exist.
- **w**: Open for writing. Creates a new file or truncates an existing file.
- **a**: Open for appending. Creates a new file or writes at the end of an existing file.
- **r+**: Open for both reading and writing. The file must exist.
- **w+**: Open for both reading and writing. Creates a new file or truncates an existing file.
- **b**: Binary mode (can be combined with other modes, such as `"rb"` or `"wb"`).

Example: Opening a file for reading

```
FILE *file = fopen("data.txt", "r");
if (file == NULL) {
    perror("Error opening file");
    return 1;   // Handle error gracefully
}
```

Closing a File with `fclose()`

Once you are done working with a file, you should close it using `fclose()`. This ensures that the file is properly saved and system resources are released.

Syntax:

`int fclose(FILE *file);`

Returns:

- `0` if the file is successfully closed.
- `EOF` if an error occurs during closing.

Example:

```
fclose(file);   // Close the file after operations are done
```

1.2 Reading from Files

Once a file is opened, you can read from it using functions like `fscanf()`, `fgets()`, and `fgetc()`. These functions are designed to work with text files and handle both formatted and unformatted data.

1.2.1 `fscanf()` – Formatted Input

`fscanf()` works similarly to `scanf()`, but instead of reading input from standard input (keyboard), it reads from a file. It allows you to read formatted data from the file (such as integers, floats, strings, etc.).

Syntax:

```
int fscanf(FILE *file, const char *format, ...);
```

- **file**: The file pointer from which data is read.
- **format**: The format string, which specifies the expected format of the data in the file.

Example: Reading data from a file

```
FILE *file = fopen("data.txt", "r");
int num;
char str[100];

if (file != NULL) {
    while (fscanf(file, "%d %s", &num, str) != EOF) {
        printf("Number: %d, String: %s\n", num, str);
    }
    fclose(file);
}
```

1.2.2 fgets() – Reading a Line

fgets() is used to read an entire line from a file, including spaces, until either a newline character or the end of the file is encountered.

Syntax:

```
char *fgets(char *str, int n, FILE *file);
```

- **str**: The buffer where the line is stored.
- **n**: The maximum number of characters to read (including the null terminator).
- **file**: The file pointer.

Example: Reading a full line from a file

```c
FILE *file = fopen("data.txt", "r");
char line[256];

if (file != NULL) {
    while (fgets(line, sizeof(line), file)) {
        printf("Read line: %s", line);
    }
    fclose(file);
}
```

1.2.3 fgetc() – Reading a Single Character

fgetc() reads a single character from the file. It is often used for character-by-character processing.

Syntax:

```c
int fgetc(FILE *file);
```

- **Returns**: The character read, or EOF if the end of file is reached or if an error occurs.

Example: Reading a file character by character

```c
FILE *file = fopen("data.txt", "r");
int ch;

if (file != NULL) {
    while ((ch = fgetc(file)) != EOF) {
        putchar(ch);   // Output each character to the console
    }
    fclose(file);
}
```

1.3 Writing to Files

Writing to files in C can be done using fprintf(), fputs(), and fwrite(). These functions allow you to write formatted text, strings, and binary data to files.

1.3.1 fprintf() – Formatted Output

`fprintf()` is used to write formatted data to a file, much like `printf()` writes to the console.

Syntax:

```
int fprintf(FILE *file, const char *format, ...);
```

- **file**: The file pointer to which data is written.
- **format**: The format string that specifies how to format the output.

Example: Writing formatted data to a file

```
FILE *file = fopen("output.txt", "w");
if (file != NULL) {
    int num = 42;
    fprintf(file, "The number is: %d\n", num);
    fclose(file);
}
```

1.3.2 fputs() – Writing a String

`fputs()` writes a string to a file without formatting.

Syntax:

```
int fputs(const char *str, FILE *file);
```

Example: Writing a string to a file

```
FILE *file = fopen("output.txt", "w");
if (file != NULL) {
    fputs("Hello, world!\n", file);
    fclose(file);
}
```

1.3.3 fwrite() – Writing Binary Data

`fwrite()` is used to write binary data to a file, making it ideal for writing data structures, arrays, or raw data in binary form.

Syntax:

```
size_t fwrite(const void *ptr, size_t size, size_t count, FILE *file);
```

- `ptr`: The pointer to the data to be written.
- `size`: The size of each element to be written.
- `count`: The number of elements to write.

Example: Writing an array of integers to a binary file

```
FILE *file = fopen("data.bin", "wb");
int numbers[] = {1, 2, 3, 4, 5};

if (file != NULL) {
    fwrite(numbers, sizeof(int), 5, file);  // Write 5 integers to the binary file
    fclose(file);
}
```

2. Error Handling in File I/O

Error handling is critical when working with files, as file operations are prone to failure due to reasons such as missing files, insufficient permissions, full disk space, or hardware failures. C provides several ways to detect and handle file errors.

2.1 Checking for Errors after Opening a File

The first thing to check when working with files is whether the file was successfully opened. If `fopen()` returns `NULL`, it means the file could not be opened.

Example:

```
FILE *file = fopen("data.txt", "r");
if (file == NULL) {
    perror("Error opening file");
    return 1;   // Gracefully handle the error
}
```

`perror()` prints a descriptive error message based on the global `errno` variable.

2.2 Checking for Read/Write Errors

When reading or writing data, functions like `fscanf()`, `fgets()`, and `fwrite()` may fail. You should check their return values to detect such errors.

For instance, `fscanf()` returns the number of successfully matched and assigned items, while `fwrite()` returns the number of items successfully written.

Example:

```
int num;
FILE *file = fopen("data.txt", "r");

if (file != NULL) {
    if (fscanf(file, "%d", &num) != 1) {
        printf("Error reading data\n");
    }
    fclose(file);
}
```

2.3 Checking for End of File (EOF)

When reading a file, you can use `feof()` to check if the end of the file has been reached. This is particularly useful when reading data in a loop.

Example:

```
FILE *file = fopen("data.txt", "r");
char line[100];

if (file != NULL) {
    while (!feof(file)) {
        if (fgets(line, sizeof(line), file)) {
            printf("Read line: %s", line);
        }
    }
    fclose(file);
}
```

3. Conclusion

File I/O in C is a powerful mechanism for reading from and writing to files. Understanding functions like `fopen()`, `fclose()`, `fscanf()`, `fprintf()`, `fread()`, and `fwrite()` enables you to handle both text and binary files with ease. Proper error handling—through checks after file operations, using `perror()`, and monitoring for EOF—ensures your program can gracefully handle errors such as file not found, read/write failures, and permission issues.

By following best practices such as checking for successful file opening, ensuring proper file closure, handling errors promptly, and using the appropriate function for text versus binary files, you can write robust, efficient file handling code in C. Mastering these file I/O techniques is crucial for building real-world applications that require persistent data storage, logging, and complex data manipulation.

11: Debugging and Best Practices

- **Common Errors in C**
    - Syntax errors, runtime errors, and logical errors.
- **Using the Debugger (GDB)**
    - Introduction to GDB: setting breakpoints, stepping through code, inspecting variables.
- **Best Coding Practices**
    - Code style, indentation, and readability.
    - Writing reusable and maintainable code.

11 DEBUGGING AND BEST PRACTICES

Debugging is often regarded as the process of identifying, analyzing, and fixing errors in your code. In C programming, debugging becomes especially critical due to the language's low-level nature and the fact that it offers direct memory manipulation. Without the right tools and practices, C programs can easily become complex, hard to maintain, and error-prone. This chapter will introduce common errors you might encounter, demonstrate how to use debugging tools like **GDB (GNU Debugger)**, and guide you on best coding practices to write clean, efficient, and maintainable code.

1. Common Errors in C

There are three primary categories of errors in C programming: **syntax errors**, **runtime errors**, and **logical errors**. Understanding how to identify and resolve each of these errors will improve your debugging skills and help you develop more robust software.

1.1 Syntax Errors

Syntax errors occur when the program doesn't follow the rules of the C language. These errors are typically identified at compile time and are usually simple to fix because the compiler gives clear feedback on where the error occurred.

- **Missing or misplaced semicolons**: Every statement in C must end with a semicolon. Forgetting it will result in a syntax error.

    Example:

    ```
    int a = 5   // Missing semicolon causes syntax error
    ```

    Fix:

    ```
    int a = 5;  // Correct
    ```

- **Mismatched parentheses or braces**: You must ensure that every opening parenthesis (, bracket [, or brace { has a corresponding closing counterpart. This is a common mistake in larger blocks of code or when nesting functions or control structures.

    Example:

    ```
    if (x > 0 {  // Mismatched parentheses
        printf("Positive number\n");
    }
    ```

    Fix:

    ```
    if (x > 0) {  // Correct
        printf("Positive number\n");
    }
    ```

- **Typographical errors in keywords or identifiers**: C is case-sensitive, so int and Int are treated as different identifiers. Misspelling keywords or variable names can result in errors.

    Example:

    ```
    in main() {  // Incorrect spelling of 'int'
        printf("Hello\n");
    }
    ```

Fix:

```
int main() {  // Correct spelling of 'int'
    printf("Hello\n");
}
```

1.2 Runtime Errors

Unlike syntax errors, **runtime errors** occur while the program is running. These errors are typically more difficult to catch because they might not appear in every execution. They often arise from unforeseen circumstances, such as invalid input or memory-related issues.

- **Segmentation faults (segfaults)**: This is one of the most common runtime errors. A segfault occurs when the program attempts to access memory it shouldn't—either by dereferencing a NULL pointer, going out of bounds of an array, or accessing freed memory.

    Example:

    ```
    int *ptr = NULL;
    *ptr = 10;  // Dereferencing a NULL pointer
    ```

    Fix:

    ```
    if (ptr != NULL) {
        *ptr = 10;  // Always check pointers before dereferencing
    }
    ```

- **Memory allocation errors**: Allocating memory dynamically using `malloc()`, `calloc()`, or `realloc()` can fail due to reasons like insufficient memory. This can lead to unpredictable behavior if you don't check whether memory allocation was successful.

Example:

```
int *arr = (int*) malloc(100 * sizeof(int));  //
Memory allocation without checking success
```

Fix:

```
int *arr = (int*) malloc(100 * sizeof(int));
if (arr == NULL) {
    fprintf(stderr, "Memory allocation failed\n");
    exit(1);  // Handle allocation failure
}
```

- **Division by zero**: This occurs when you attempt to divide a number by zero. It leads to undefined behavior.

Example:

```
int x = 10, y = 0;
int result = x / y;  // Division by zero error
```

Fix:

```
if (y != 0) {
    int result = x / y;
} else {
    fprintf(stderr, "Error: Division by zero\n");
}
```

1.3 Logical Errors

Logical errors are the hardest to identify and fix because the code compiles and runs without crashing, but it doesn't produce the correct results. These errors arise from mistakes in the logic of your algorithms.

- **Incorrect conditionals**: Sometimes, a condition in an `if` statement may be logically incorrect, leading to wrong program flow or unexpected behavior.

Example:

```
int isEven(int num) {
    return num % 2 == 1;  // Incorrect logic; it should check for even, not odd
}
```

Fix

```
int isEven(int num) {
    return num % 2 == 0;  // Correct logic
}
```

- **Off-by-one errors**: A common mistake when dealing with arrays and loops, especially when managing indices. For example, iterating through an array from 0 to n when the array's indices are from 0 to n-1.

Example:

```
for (int i = 0; i <= n; i++) {  // Off-by-one error; should be i < n
    printf("%d\n", arr[i]);
}
```

Fix:

```
for (int i = 0; i < n; i++) {  // Correct loop condition
    printf("%d\n", arr[i]);
}
```

2. Using the Debugger (GDB)

Debugging is a crucial skill for developers. Tools like **GDB** (GNU Debugger) provide powerful features for tracing and diagnosing issues within your code. GDB allows you to set breakpoints, step through your program line by line, inspect variables, and backtrack from a crash (e.g., a segmentation fault).

2.1 Introduction to GDB

GDB is a command-line debugger that helps you track down errors, inspect your program's state during execution, and understand what's going wrong.

Setting Up GDB

1. **Compile your code with debugging information**: This allows GDB to map the source code to the compiled machine code, making debugging more understandable.

   Example:

   ```
   gcc -g -o myprogram myprogram.c
   ```

2. **Start GDB**: To run your program inside GDB, use:

   ```
   gdb ./myprogram
   ```

3. **Set breakpoints**: A breakpoint is a point in the program where GDB will stop execution. You can set breakpoints at specific lines of code or at function calls.

   Example:

   ```
   (gdb) break main   // Break at the start of the
   main function
   ```

4. **Running your program**: After setting breakpoints, you can start running the program inside GDB:

   ```
   (gdb) run
   ```

5. **Inspecting variables**: You can use GDB to print the values of variables at specific points during execution.

Example:

```
(gdb) print myVariable
```

6. **Stepping through code**: After a breakpoint is hit, you can step through the program line by line to observe the flow of execution.
    - `step`: Executes the current line and steps into any functions called on that line.
    - `next`: Executes the current line, but steps over any function calls.
    - `continue`: Resumes execution until the next breakpoint is encountered.

Example:

```
(gdb) next    // Step to the next line
```

7. **Backtrace on crash**: If your program crashes (e.g., due to a segmentation fault), GDB can show you the **backtrace**—a list of function calls leading up to the crash. This is especially useful for tracking down memory access errors.

Example:

```
(gdb) backtrace   // Show the call stack at the point of the crash
```

8. **Exiting GDB**: To exit GDB, use:

```
(gdb) quit
```

3. Best Coding Practices

Writing clean and maintainable code is essential, especially for larger projects or projects that require collaboration with other developers. Good coding practices improve code readability, reduce errors, and make the codebase easier to extend or modify.

3.1 Code Style and Readability

- **Consistent indentation**: Proper indentation helps to visually represent the program's structure. Most developers use 2 or 4 spaces per indentation level. Avoid using tabs in place of spaces for consistency.

    Example:

    ```
    if (condition) {
        printf("Condition is true\n");
    }
    ```

- **Descriptive naming**: Use meaningful names for variables, functions, and constants. Avoid generic names like `temp`, `var`, or `data`. Instead, use names that convey the purpose of the variable.

    Example:

    ```
    int totalPrice = 100;
    float discountRate = 0.10;
    ```

- **Commenting your code**: Comments should explain why a block of code is written a certain way, not what it does. Write comments for complex algorithms or decisions, but avoid obvious comments.

    Good example:

    ```
    // Apply a discount to the total price
    totalPrice -= totalPrice * discountRate;
    ```

    Bad example:

    ```
    // Set total price to 100
    totalPrice = 100;  // This is unnecessary
    ```

3.2 Writing Reusable and Maintainable Code

- **Modular design**: Break your code into smaller, reusable functions. Each function should ideally perform one task, improving readability and reducing redundancy.

    Example:

    ```
    float calculateDiscount(float price, float rate)
    {
        return price * rate;
    }
    ```

- **Avoid hardcoding values**: Instead of hardcoding constant values throughout your code, define them as constants or configuration settings. This makes your code easier to modify and understand.

    Example:

    ```
    #define MAX_SIZE 100   // Use constants instead of magic numbers
    ```

- **Error handling**: Always handle potential errors such as invalid input, memory allocation failures, or file I/O errors. Use proper error messages and return values to help debug issues quickly.

    Example:

    ```
    if (ptr == NULL) {
        fprintf(stderr, "Memory allocation failed\n");
        exit(1);
    }
    ```

- **Consistent formatting**: Maintain a consistent formatting style across your codebase. This includes naming conventions, brace placement, and indentation style.

4. Conclusion

Debugging is a skill that every C programmer needs to master. By understanding the different types of errors—syntax errors, runtime errors, and logical errors—and learning how to use tools like **GDB**, you can become proficient in finding and fixing bugs in your code.

Equally important is writing clean, maintainable code. By adhering to best practices like consistent indentation, meaningful variable names, modular design, and proper error handling, you will write code that is not only easier to debug but also easier to read, maintain, and extend.

By mastering both debugging techniques and coding best practices, you can significantly improve the quality of your code and become a more effective C programmer.

12: Your First C Project

- **Designing a Simple C Program**
    - Planning, designing, and implementing a simple project (e.g., a simple calculator, a to-do list, etc.).
- **Testing and Debugging the Program**
    - Debugging and fixing common issues.
- **Compiling and Running the Program**
    - How to compile and run a C program from the command line.

12 YOUR FIRST C PROJECT

Building your first project is a significant milestone in any programming journey. It consolidates everything you have learned so far, from understanding basic syntax to handling variables, loops, functions, and memory management. In this chapter, we will walk through the process of **designing**, **implementing**, **testing**, and **debugging** a simple C project. By the end of the chapter, you'll not only have a fully functional project but also an understanding of how to approach real-world programming challenges.

For our project, we will design and implement a **simple calculator** program. This project will involve basic input/output, decision-making with `if` statements, loops, and functions.

1. Designing a Simple C Program

Before jumping into coding, it's essential to **plan and design** the structure of the program. Designing your program first helps you organize your thoughts, identify potential challenges, and set a clear direction for implementation.

1.1 Planning the Project

Let's break down the design process step by step:

1. **Objective of the Project**:
   The goal of this project is to create a simple calculator program that can perform basic arithmetic operations (addition, subtraction, multiplication, division).
2. **Input/Output**:
   - The program will take two numbers as input from the user.
   - The user will then choose the operation to perform (addition, subtraction, multiplication, or division).
   - The program will output the result of the chosen operation.
3. **Functional Requirements**:
   - The calculator should support basic arithmetic operations: +, -, *, /.
   - The program should handle invalid input, such as non-numeric data or division by zero.
   - The program should allow the user to perform multiple calculations without restarting the program (i.e., the user can choose to perform another operation or exit).
4. **Non-Functional Requirements**:
   - The program should be fast, easy to use, and handle errors gracefully.
   - It should be written in a modular fashion, making the code easy to extend in the future (e.g., adding more operations or improving the user interface).

1.2 Designing the Program Structure

The next step in the design process is deciding how to structure the code. In our case, the program is small, so we can get by with a simple design.

- **Functions**: We will create separate functions for each operation (e.g., `add()`, `subtract()`, `multiply()`, `divide()`) and a function to display the menu and handle user input.
- **Variables**: We'll need variables to store the two numbers entered by the user and the result of the operation.
- **Control Flow**: The program will use loops and `if` statements to keep the calculator running and ensure valid user input.

1.3 Example Flowchart

A flowchart is a useful tool to visualize the logic before coding. Here's a simple flowchart for the calculator:

1. Start.
2. Display the menu with options for the user.
3. Ask the user for the first number.
4. Ask the user for the second number.
5. Ask the user to choose the operation.
6. Perform the operation and display the result.
7. Ask the user if they want to perform another calculation.
8. If yes, repeat from step 3.
9. If no, exit.

1.4 Writing Pseudocode

Pseudocode helps break down the logic further without worrying about syntax. Here's an outline:

```
START
    Display Menu
    Get first number from user
    Get second number from user
    Display operation choices (+, -, *, /)
    Get operation choice from user
    If operation is valid:
        Perform operation
        Display result
    Else:
        Display "Invalid operation"
    Ask user if they want to perform another operation
    If yes, repeat
    If no, exit
END
```

This pseudocode serves as the blueprint for your C program.

2. Implementing the Program

Now that we have a solid design, we can start writing the C code for our calculator.

```c
#include <stdio.h>

// Function declarations
void add(float num1, float num2);
void subtract(float num1, float num2);
void multiply(float num1, float num2);
void divide(float num1, float num2);
void displayMenu();

int main() {
    float num1, num2;
    int choice;

    do {
        displayMenu();
        printf("Enter your choice (1/2/3/4): ");
```

```c
        scanf("%d", &choice);

        if (choice < 1 || choice > 4) {
            printf("Invalid choice. Please try again.\n");
            continue;  // Skip the rest and ask for input again
        }

        printf("Enter the first number: ");
        scanf("%f", &num1);
        printf("Enter the second number: ");
        scanf("%f", &num2);

        switch (choice) {
            case 1:
                add(num1, num2);
                break;
            case 2:
                subtract(num1, num2);
                break;
            case 3:
                multiply(num1, num2);
                break;
            case 4:
                if (num2 == 0) {
                    printf("Error: Division by zero is not allowed.\n");
                } else {
                    divide(num1, num2);
                }
                break;
            default:
                printf("Invalid operation.\n");
        }

        printf("Do you want to perform another calculation? (1 = Yes, 0 = No): ");
        scanf("%d", &choice);

    } while (choice == 1);

    printf("Goodbye!\n");
    return 0;
}

// Function definitions
```

```c
void add(float num1, float num2) {
    printf("Result: %.2f\n", num1 + num2);
}

void subtract(float num1, float num2) {
    printf("Result: %.2f\n", num1 - num2);
}

void multiply(float num1, float num2) {
    printf("Result: %.2f\n", num1 * num2);
}

void divide(float num1, float num2) {
    printf("Result: %.2f\n", num1 / num2);
}

void displayMenu() {
    printf("\nSimple Calculator\n");
    printf("1. Add\n");
    printf("2. Subtract\n");
    printf("3. Multiply\n");
    printf("4. Divide\n");
}
```

Explanation of the Code:

- **Function Definitions**: We created separate functions for each operation (`add()`, `subtract()`, `multiply()`, and `divide()`) that take two `float` arguments (the numbers to operate on) and print the result.
- **Menu System**: The program displays a menu prompting the user to choose an operation. If the user inputs an invalid operation, the program asks them to try again.
- **Input Handling**: The program uses `scanf` to get user input for numbers and operation choice. It performs input validation where necessary (e.g., preventing division by zero).
- **Looping**: After completing one calculation, the program asks the user if they want to perform another operation. If the user answers "yes" (1), the program continues; otherwise, it exits.

3. Testing and Debugging the Program

After implementing the program, the next step is testing. It's essential to test the program with different inputs to ensure it behaves as expected.

3.1 Testing the Program

Test the program with various inputs:

1. **Valid Inputs**:
   - Test with valid operations, like `1 + 2`, `5 - 3`, `4 * 2`, and `8 / 2`.
   - Test with decimal numbers, e.g., `4.5 + 2.5`, `7.8 - 2.4`.
2. **Invalid Inputs**:
   - Input non-numeric values (e.g., letters instead of numbers).
   - Try division by zero (`4 / 0`) to verify the error handling.
   - Test for invalid operation choices (e.g., choosing option 5 when only 1-4 are valid).
3. **Edge Cases**:
   - Test with very large or very small numbers to ensure the program handles them correctly.
   - Test repeated operations (e.g., multiple calculations in one session).

3.2 Debugging Common Issues

Here are some common issues you might encounter and how to fix them:

1. **Incorrect Calculation**:
   - Ensure that each operation (addition, subtraction, multiplication, division) is implemented correctly and that the correct function is called in the `switch` statement.

2. **Segmentation Fault**:
   - This could occur if you try to access uninitialized variables or improper memory handling (though this is less common in this simple program). If using pointers or arrays, always ensure bounds are respected.
3. **Invalid Input Handling**:
   - If the program crashes or behaves unpredictably when non-numeric input is entered, make sure you handle invalid input correctly. You may want to check that the input is a valid number using `scanf` or by clearing the input buffer after each read.

3.3 Using Debugging Tools

You can use **GDB (GNU Debugger)** or even print statements to debug the program. For example, placing `printf` statements inside your functions can help you understand the flow of the program and check whether the values are being correctly passed to the functions.

4. Compiling and Running the Program

Now that we have the program ready, let's go over how to compile and run it from the command line.

4.1 Compiling the Program

To compile a C program, you need to use the C compiler (`gcc` in most systems). Assuming your program is saved in a file called `calculator.c`, open your terminal or command prompt and use the following command:

```
gcc -o calculator calculator.c
```

Here:

- `gcc`: The GNU Compiler Collection (C compiler).
- `-o calculator`: Tells the compiler to output the compiled code as an executable named `calculator`.
- `calculator.c`: The name of the source code file.

4.2 Running the Program

Once the program is compiled, you can run it from the command line by typing:

```
./calculator
```

This will launch your calculator program. Follow the on-screen prompts to test the functionality.

5. Conclusion

In this chapter, we've successfully designed and implemented a simple calculator program in C. You learned how to approach a project by planning the design, breaking it down into smaller tasks, and then writing modular code. We also covered testing and debugging, ensuring that your program works as expected, and how to compile and run your C programs.

This is just the beginning of your journey with C programming. As you gain more experience, you can extend your projects to more complex applications, implementing advanced features, and utilizing libraries to make your programs even more powerful.

Your First C Real time Project

Creating real-time, practical projects is a great way to solidify your understanding of programming concepts and develop problem-solving skills. In this chapter, we'll take a deeper dive into building a **real-time project** using C, focusing on the process of planning, designing, implementing, testing, debugging, and running the project. We will guide you through a **To-Do List Application**, a commonly used program that showcases multiple concepts including file I/O, dynamic memory allocation, and user interaction.

1. Designing a Real-Time C Program

When developing a real-world program, the design process is essential. A well-designed program is easy to maintain, extend, and debug. We will walk through how to design and plan the architecture for a simple **To-Do List Application** that allows the user to:

- Add new tasks to the list.
- Display all tasks.
- Mark tasks as completed.
- Delete tasks.
- Save and load the list from a file.

1.1 Planning the Project

Before starting any code, it's crucial to first identify the requirements and plan the structure of the application. For a **To-Do List Application**, here are the key points we need to consider:

1. **Features**:
    - Add tasks: The user can input a task (description).
    - List tasks: Display all tasks with their status (pending or completed).
    - Mark tasks as completed: Update a task's status.
    - Delete tasks: Remove a task from the list.
    - Save the list: Persist tasks in a file so that they can be accessed later.
    - Load the list: Read tasks from the file when the program starts.
2. **Input and Output**:
    - **Input:** The program will accept user commands via a text-based menu (e.g., 1 for adding a task, 2 for viewing tasks).
    - **Output:** The program will print the current list of tasks to the terminal, showing task descriptions and their statuses.
3. **Data Representation**:
    - We will represent each task as a structure (`struct`) with fields for the task description and a flag indicating whether the task is completed.
    - The tasks will be stored in a dynamic array (using pointers) that will expand as new tasks are added.
4. **File Handling**:
    - The program will read from and write to a file to store the list of tasks. This will allow the user to close and reopen the program without losing data.

1.2 Defining the Program Structure

For this application, we'll design it in a modular fashion, separating logic into functions to maintain clarity and ease of modification.

Core Functions:

- `addTask()`: Adds a new task to the list.
- `displayTasks()`: Displays all tasks (pending or completed).
- `deleteTask()`: Deletes a task by its index.
- `markTaskCompleted()`: Marks a specific task as completed.
- `saveToFile()`: Saves the current task list to a file.
- `loadFromFile()`: Loads tasks from the file when the program starts.

Data Structures:

- We will use a `struct` to represent each task and an array (or dynamically allocated memory) to store the tasks.

Example struct:

```c
typedef struct {
    char description[256];
    int isCompleted;
} Task;
```

We can store a list of `Task` structs dynamically using a pointer and resize it as needed.

2. Implementing the Program

Now that we have the design in place, we can begin implementing the project in C.

2.1 Code Implementation

```c
#include <stdio.h>
#include <stdlib.h>
#include <string.h>

// Define the Task structure
typedef struct {
    char description[256];
    int isCompleted;
} Task;

// Function prototypes
void addTask(Task **tasks, int *taskCount);
void displayTasks(Task *tasks, int taskCount);
void deleteTask(Task **tasks, int *taskCount, int index);
void markTaskCompleted(Task *tasks, int taskCount, int index);
void saveToFile(Task *tasks, int taskCount);
void loadFromFile(Task **tasks, int *taskCount);

int main() {
    Task *tasks = NULL;
    int taskCount = 0;
    int choice;

    // Load tasks from file at the start of the program
    loadFromFile(&tasks, &taskCount);

    do {
        printf("\nTo-Do List Application\n");
        printf("1. Add Task\n");
        printf("2. View Tasks\n");
        printf("3. Mark Task as Completed\n");
        printf("4. Delete Task\n");
        printf("5. Exit\n");
        printf("Enter your choice: ");
        scanf("%d", &choice);
        getchar(); // to consume the newline left by scanf
```

```c
        switch (choice) {
            case 1:
                addTask(&tasks, &taskCount);
                break;
            case 2:
                displayTasks(tasks, taskCount);
                break;
            case 3: {
                int index;
                printf("Enter task number to mark as completed: ");
                scanf("%d", &index);
                markTaskCompleted(tasks, taskCount, index - 1);   // Index is user-friendly (1-based)
                break;
            }
            case 4: {
                int index;
                printf("Enter task number to delete: ");
                scanf("%d", &index);
                deleteTask(&tasks, &taskCount, index - 1);   // Index is user-friendly (1-based)
                break;
            }
            case 5:
                // Save tasks before exiting
                saveToFile(tasks, taskCount);
                printf("Goodbye!\n");
                break;
            default:
                printf("Invalid choice. Please try again.\n");
        }
    } while (choice != 5);

    // Free allocated memory before exiting
    free(tasks);
    return 0;
}

// Function to add a task
void addTask(Task **tasks, int *taskCount) {
    Task newTask;
    printf("Enter task description: ");
    fgets(newTask.description, 256, stdin);
```

```c
    newTask.description[strcspn(newTask.description,
"\n")] = '\0';  // Remove newline character
    newTask.isCompleted = 0;

    // Resize the array to fit the new task
    *tasks = realloc(*tasks, (*taskCount + 1) *
sizeof(Task));
    if (*tasks == NULL) {
        printf("Memory allocation failed.\n");
        exit(1);
    }

    // Add the new task
    (*tasks)[*taskCount] = newTask;
    (*taskCount)++;
    printf("Task added successfully.\n");
}

// Function to display all tasks
void displayTasks(Task *tasks, int taskCount) {
    if (taskCount == 0) {
        printf("No tasks available.\n");
        return;
    }

    printf("\nTasks:\n");
    for (int i = 0; i < taskCount; i++) {
        printf("%d. %s [%s]\n", i + 1,
tasks[i].description, tasks[i].isCompleted ?
"Completed" : "Pending");
    }
}

// Function to mark a task as completed
void markTaskCompleted(Task *tasks, int taskCount, int
index) {
    if (index < 0 || index >= taskCount) {
        printf("Invalid task index.\n");
        return;
    }

    tasks[index].isCompleted = 1;
    printf("Task marked as completed.\n");
}

// Function to delete a task
```

```c
void deleteTask(Task **tasks, int *taskCount, int index) {
    if (index < 0 || index >= *taskCount) {
        printf("Invalid task index.\n");
        return;
    }

    // Shift tasks down to fill the gap
    for (int i = index; i < *taskCount - 1; i++) {
        (*tasks)[i] = (*tasks)[i + 1];
    }

    // Resize the array
    *tasks = realloc(*tasks, (*taskCount - 1) * sizeof(Task));
    if (*tasks == NULL && *taskCount > 1) {
        printf("Memory allocation failed.\n");
        exit(1);
    }

    (*taskCount)--;
    printf("Task deleted successfully.\n");
}

// Function to save tasks to a file
void saveToFile(Task *tasks, int taskCount) {
    FILE *file = fopen("tasks.txt", "w");
    if (file == NULL) {
        printf("Error opening file for saving tasks.\n");
        return;
    }

    for (int i = 0; i < taskCount; i++) {
        fprintf(file, "%s\n%d\n", tasks[i].description, tasks[i].isCompleted);
    }

    fclose(file);
    printf("Tasks saved to file.\n");
}

// Function to load tasks from a file
void loadFromFile(Task **tasks, int *taskCount) {
    FILE *file = fopen("tasks.txt", "r");
    if (file == NULL) {
```

```c
        return;  // No tasks file exists, we start with an empty list
    }

    Task task;
    while (fscanf(file, "%255[^\n]\n%d\n", task.description, &task.isCompleted) != EOF) {
        *tasks = realloc(*tasks, (*taskCount + 1) * sizeof(Task));
        if (*tasks == NULL) {
            printf("Memory allocation failed.\n");
            exit(1);
        }
        (*tasks)[*taskCount] = task;
        (*taskCount)++;
    }

    fclose(file);
    printf("Tasks loaded from file.\n");
}
```

3. Testing and Debugging the Program

After implementing the program, it's time to test it thoroughly.

3.1 Testing the Features

- **Adding Tasks**: Check if new tasks are correctly added to the list. Ensure the task description is stored properly and that it can be viewed.
- **Displaying Tasks**: Ensure all tasks, including their statuses (completed or pending), are displayed correctly.
- **Marking Tasks as Completed**: Verify that tasks can be marked as completed and the status is updated accordingly.
- **Deleting Tasks**: Test that tasks can be deleted and the list updates correctly.
- **Saving and Loading**: Ensure tasks are saved to a file correctly and that the program loads tasks properly when restarted.

3.2 Debugging Common Issues

1. **Memory Management**:
   - Ensure that you are properly managing memory by using `malloc` and `realloc` to resize the task array.
   - Avoid memory leaks by freeing the allocated memory (`free(tasks)`) before exiting.
2. **File I/O**:
   - Make sure the program opens the file for reading and writing without errors.
   - Ensure correct formatting when saving and loading tasks, including handling of newline characters.
3. **User Input Validation**:
   - Handle invalid user inputs gracefully, such as entering non-numeric choices for menu options or providing invalid task indices.

3.3 Using GDB for Debugging

If you encounter errors, you can use **GDB** to set breakpoints, inspect variables, and step through the code. For example:

1. Compile the program with debugging symbols:

   ```
   gcc -g -o todo todo.c
   ```

2. Start GDB:

   ```
   gdb ./todo
   ```

3. Set breakpoints, e.g., at the `addTask()` function:

   ```
   break addTask
   run
   ```

4. Step through the code, check variable values, and diagnose any issues.

4. Compiling and Running the Program

4.1 Compiling

To compile the program from the command line:

```
gcc -o todo todo.c
```
4.2 Running

Run the compiled program:

```
./todo
```

Test the functionality by following the on-screen prompts to add, delete, mark, and view tasks.

5. Conclusion

In this chapter, we've walked through the process of designing and implementing a **To-Do List Application** in C. You've learned how to:

- Design a real-world application.
- Break down the logic into smaller, manageable functions.
- Handle dynamic memory allocation and file I/O.
- Test and debug the program to ensure its robustness.

This project serves as a great foundation for understanding how C can be used to build practical, real-time applications. With this knowledge, you can expand this program further or start new projects involving more complex data structures, algorithms, and features.

Additional Resources

As you continue your journey into learning C programming and software development, it's important to take advantage of a wealth of online resources, communities, and books that can provide valuable insights, tips, and practical examples. Whether you're just starting or aiming to deepen your knowledge, the following list includes some of the best places to learn, ask questions, and explore advanced topics in C.

1. Useful Online Resources

There is no shortage of online platforms that offer tutorials, documentation, discussion forums, and interactive learning experiences. Below are some of the top online resources to enhance your understanding of C programming:

1.1. Official Documentation and Standards

1. **ISO/IEC Standard for C (ISO/IEC 9899)**
   - While the full standard can be dense, the official documentation is an essential reference for understanding the language's syntax, semantics, and best practices. It's available for purchase from the ISO website, but you may find summaries and discussions about it online as well.
   - Link: ISO/IEC 9899:2018
2. **C Programming Wiki (C Programming Language Reference)**
   - A good reference for C syntax, functions, keywords, and library functions. It is organized and easy to navigate, providing examples and explanations.
   - Link: C Programming Wiki

1.2. Online Courses and Tutorials

1. **Udemy: C Programming For Beginners – Master the C Language**
   - A highly-rated course on Udemy that covers the basics of C programming, structured for beginners. It also includes hands-on coding exercises and examples.
   - Link: Udemy - C Programming for Beginners
2. **Coursera – Introduction to C Programming (University of California, Santa Cruz)**
   - A comprehensive online course that covers C programming fundamentals with a focus on algorithms and data structures.
   - Link: Coursera C Programming
3. **edX: C Programming with Linux (Linux Foundation)**
   - This free online course provides an introduction to C programming with a focus on Linux systems. It covers system-level programming, which is often a key area for advanced C programmers.
   - Link: edX C Programming with Linux

1.3. Coding Practice Websites

1. **LeetCode**
   - LeetCode offers hundreds of algorithmic challenges, many of which can be solved using C. It's an excellent way to practice problem-solving skills in C.
   - Link: LeetCode
2. **HackerRank**
   - HackerRank provides coding challenges in various domains, including algorithms, data structures, and specific C programming challenges.
   - Link: HackerRank C Challenges
3. **Codeforces**
   - Codeforces is a competitive programming platform that hosts programming contests and challenges. You can practice problems written in C and other languages.
   - Link: Codeforces

4. **Exercism.io**
   - Exercism offers hands-on programming practice with mentorship. The C track offers well-structured exercises to help you master the language.
   - Link: Exercism C Track

1.4. C Programming Tutorials

1. **GeeksforGeeks**
   - GeeksforGeeks is a comprehensive resource that provides tutorials, articles, and problems to help programmers understand core concepts in C and other languages.
   - Link: GeeksforGeeks C Programming
2. **TutorialsPoint**
   - TutorialsPoint offers a wide range of beginner-friendly tutorials on C programming. It includes examples and detailed explanations on topics like arrays, pointers, structures, and file I/O.
   - Link: TutorialsPoint C Programming
3. **The C Programming Language – Tutorial (by Brian Kernighan and Dennis Ritchie)**
   - While not an official tutorial site, many websites host tutorials based on the famous book "The C Programming Language" by Brian Kernighan and Dennis Ritchie (often referred to as K&R). The book remains one of the most authoritative texts on C and continues to be a reference point for many tutorials.
   - Link: The C Programming Language

1.5. C Language Forums and Communities

1. **Stack Overflow**
   - Stack Overflow is an essential resource where programmers can ask and answer questions related to C programming. It is particularly useful for troubleshooting specific issues in your code.
   - Link: Stack Overflow C Programming Questions

2. **Reddit – r/C_Programming**
    - The C Programming subreddit is a community of C programmers where you can share resources, ask questions, and discuss anything related to C programming.
    - Link: r/C_Programming
3. **Cprogramming.com Forums**
    - This forum is specifically dedicated to discussions about C and C++ programming, with sections for beginners and advanced topics.
    - Link: Cprogramming.com Forums
4. **The C Programming Language Forum (StackExchange)**
    - This forum is part of the larger StackExchange network and is dedicated to C programming. It's a great place to ask specific questions about C language nuances.
    - Link: StackExchange – C Programming

2. Suggested Books and Tutorials for Deeper Learning

While online resources are excellent for quick learning and reference, books can provide in-depth understanding and a more structured approach to mastering C. Below are some of the most respected books and tutorials for advancing your C programming knowledge.

2.1. Books for Beginners and Intermediate Learners

1. **"The C Programming Language" by Brian Kernighan and Dennis Ritchie (K&R)**
    - This is the definitive book on C, written by the creators of the language. It covers the syntax and features of C in a clear, concise manner, with many practical examples. If you only read one book about C, this should be the one.
    - Link: The C Programming Language (K&R)

2. **"C Programming: A Modern Approach" by K. N. King**
   - A comprehensive, clear, and well-structured book that takes you through the fundamental and advanced features of the C language. It's particularly good for people who are newer to programming.
   - Link: C Programming: A Modern Approach
3. **"Head First C" by David Griffiths and Dawn Griffiths**
   - This book offers a unique approach to teaching C through interactive exercises and illustrations. It's designed for beginners but also touches on some advanced concepts.
   - Link: Head First C
4. **"C in Depth" by Deepali Srivastava**
   - A great book for programmers who have a basic understanding of C and want to deepen their knowledge. It covers a range of topics, from arrays and pointers to complex data structures and memory management.
   - Link: C in Depth

2.2. Books for Advanced Learners

1. **"Expert C Programming: Deep C Secrets" by Peter van der Linden**
   - This book is excellent for intermediate to advanced C programmers. It goes beyond the basics, discussing subtle aspects of the language and offering a deeper understanding of C's capabilities.
   - Link: Expert C Programming
2. **"C Programming in Linux" by David Haskins**
   - If you're interested in programming for Linux, this book teaches C in the context of developing Linux applications, handling processes, memory management, and using system calls.
   - Link: C Programming in Linux
3. **"Advanced C Programming" by Peter G. Neumark**
   - This is an excellent book for advanced C programmers who want to master the intricacies of the language, including the best practices for writing efficient and portable code.
   - Link: Advanced C Programming

2.3. Tutorials for Advanced Topics

1. **"Algorithms in C" by Robert Sedgewick**
   - If you want to go beyond the basics of C programming, "Algorithms in C" is a great resource for learning advanced algorithms and data structures implemented in C.
   - Link: Algorithms in C
2. **"C Programming: A Modern Approach" by K. N. King (Advanced Sections)**
   - While this book is generally for beginners, its later chapters cover advanced topics such as file handling, dynamic memory allocation, and advanced data structures, making it a good resource for programmers who want to deepen their skills.

3. Conclusion

The journey to mastering C programming requires continuous learning and practice. By leveraging online tutorials, community discussions, coding platforms, and in-depth books, you can enhance your knowledge, sharpen your problem-solving skills, and become proficient in C programming. Remember that C is a foundational language, and a solid understanding of it will serve as a stepping stone to learning other languages and advancing your software development career. Stay curious, experiment with new projects, and immerse yourself in the vast community of C developers worldwide.

Appendix: C Programming Essentials

In this appendix, we'll provide two crucial resources for anyone learning C programming:

1. **C Syntax Cheat Sheet** – a quick reference to the essential syntax of C programming, which can help speed up your coding process and serve as a quick refresher.
2. **Glossary of Terms** – an alphabetical list of commonly used programming terms, helping to clarify jargon and provide deeper understanding of key concepts.

1. C Syntax Cheat Sheet

This cheat sheet covers the most important syntax elements, operators, functions, and concepts in C programming. It is a compact reference to have on hand while you code.

1.1. C Syntax Basics

- **Comments:**
    - Single-line comment: `// This is a comment`
    - Multi-line comment:

    ```
    /* This is a
       multi-line comment */
    ```

- **Variables and Data Types:**
    - Declare a variable: `int a;`
    - Initialize a variable: `int a = 10;`
    - Common data types:
        - `int`: Integer (whole number)
        - `float`: Floating point number
        - `char`: Single character
        - `double`: Double precision floating point number
        - `bool`: Boolean (requires `stdbool.h` header)

- **Constants:**
    o **Constant integer:** `const int max_value = 100;`
    o **Define constants:** `#define MAX_VALUE 100`

1.2. Control Structures

- **if statement:**

```
if (condition) {
    // block of code
} else {
    // block of code
}
```

- **Switch statement:**

```
switch (expression) {
    case 1:
        // block of code
        break;
    case 2:
        // block of code
        break;
    default:
        // block of code
}
```

- **Loops:**
    o **For loop:**

    ```
    for (int i = 0; i < 10; i++) {
        // block of code
    }
    ```

    o **While loop:**

    ```
    while (condition) {
        // block of code
    }
    ```

- **Do-while loop:**

  ```
  do {
      // block of code
  } while (condition);
  ```

1.3. Functions

- **Function Declaration/Definition:**

  ```
  return_type function_name(parameters) {
      // function body
  }
  ```

  Example:

  ```
  int add(int a, int b) {
      return a + b;
  }
  ```

- **Function call:**

  ```
  int result = add(5, 3);   // result is now 8
  ```

- **Function Prototypes:** A function prototype declares a function's return type and parameters before its definition.

  ```
  int add(int, int);   // Prototype
  ```

1.4. Arrays and Strings

- **Array Declaration:**

  ```
  int arr[5];   // Declares an array of 5 integers
  ```

- **Accessing Array Elements:**

  ```
  arr[0] = 10;   // First element of the array
  ```

- **String Declaration:**

  ```
  char str[] = "Hello";
  ```

- **String Manipulation Functions:**
    - `strlen(str)`: Returns length of the string.
    - `strcpy(destination, source)`: Copies string from source to destination.
    - `strcmp(str1, str2)`: Compares two strings.

1.5. Pointers

- **Pointer Declaration:**

    `int *ptr;`

- **Dereferencing a Pointer:**

    `*ptr = 5;   // Assigns 5 to the memory location pointed to by ptr`

- **Pointer Arithmetic:**

    `ptr++;   // Moves the pointer to the next memory location`

1.6. Dynamic Memory Allocation

- **malloc()** – Allocates memory dynamically.

    `int *arr = (int *)malloc(10 * sizeof(int));   // Allocates memory for an array of 10 integers`

- **free()** – Frees dynamically allocated memory.

    `free(arr);   // Frees the memory previously allocated by malloc`

- **calloc()** – Allocates memory and initializes it to zero.

    `int *arr = (int *)calloc(10, sizeof(int));   // Allocates and initializes an array of 10 integers`

1.7. File Handling

- **Opening a File:**

  ```
  FILE *file = fopen("file.txt", "r");  // Open file in read mode
  ```

- **Reading from a File:**

  ```
  char buffer[100];
  fgets(buffer, sizeof(buffer), file);  // Reads a line from the file
  ```

- **Writing to a File:**

  ```
  fprintf(file, "Hello, world!");  // Writes text to the file
  ```

- **Closing a File:**

  ```
  fclose(file);  // Closes the file
  ```

1.8. Operators

- **Arithmetic Operators:**
  - +, -, *, /, %
- **Relational Operators:**
  - ==, !=, <, >, <=, >=
- **Logical Operators:**
  - && (AND), || (OR), ! (NOT)
- **Bitwise Operators:**
  - & (AND), | (OR), ^ (XOR), ~ (NOT), << (left shift), >> (right shift)
- **Assignment Operators:**
  - =, +=, -=, *=, /=, %=

2. Glossary of Terms

Here is a list of common terms and definitions used in C programming, which will help clarify key concepts and terminology.

2.1. Common Terms

- **Array:**
    - A collection of elements of the same data type stored in contiguous memory locations. Arrays in C are zero-indexed.
- **Boolean:**
    - A data type that can hold only two values: `true` (1) or `false` (0). C doesn't have a built-in boolean type, but it can be represented using `int` with values 0 and 1. The `stdbool.h` library provides `bool`, `true`, and `false`.
- **Function:**
    - A block of code designed to perform a specific task. Functions are declared with a return type, name, and parameters, and can be invoked from other parts of the program.
- **Pointer:**
    - A variable that stores the memory address of another variable. Pointers are powerful but require careful handling, as they directly interact with memory.
- **Struct (Structure):**
    - A user-defined data type that allows grouping of variables of different types under a single name. It's used for representing complex data structures.

    ```
    struct Person {
        char name[50];
        int age;
    };
    ```

- **Dynamic Memory Allocation:**
    - The process of allocating memory during runtime using functions like `malloc()`, `calloc()`, and `realloc()`. The allocated memory must be freed with `free()`.

- **Compilation:**
    - The process of converting the source code into machine-readable code. In C, this is done using a compiler like `gcc`.
- **Stack and Heap:**
    - The **stack** is used for static memory allocation (function calls, local variables). The **heap** is used for dynamic memory allocation (using `malloc()` and similar functions).
- **Header File:**
    - A file with extension `.h` that contains function prototypes, data type definitions, and macro definitions. Common standard libraries like `stdio.h`, `stdlib.h`, and `string.h` are included via header files.
- **Preprocessor:**
    - A tool that processes code before the compiler. It handles directives like `#include`, `#define`, and conditional compilation commands like `#if` and `#endif`.
- **Segmentation Fault (Segfault):**
    - A runtime error that occurs when a program tries to access an invalid memory location. This is often caused by dereferencing invalid pointers or accessing out-of-bounds array indices.
- **Recursion:**
    - The process in which a function calls itself in order to solve a problem. Recursive functions often need a base case to stop the recursion.
- **Global Variable:**
    - A variable that is declared outside of all functions and can be accessed by any function in the program.
- **Local Variable:**
    - A variable declared within a function or block, and accessible only within that function/block.
- **Stack Overflow:**
    - An error that occurs when a program uses more stack memory than is available. This typically happens with infinite recursion or overly deep recursion.

- **Null Pointer:**
    - A pointer that doesn't point to any valid memory location. It's often used to represent the absence of a valid object.
- **Segmentation Fault (Segfault):**
    - A runtime error caused by accessing memory outside the bounds of the allocated memory. This is typically caused by invalid pointer dereferencing or out-of-bounds array access.

3. Conclusion

This appendix provides a quick reference to the most essential elements of C programming. Whether you are just starting or need a refresher, the C Syntax Cheat Sheet and Glossary of Terms will serve as valuable tools to assist in your learning process. Keep this appendix handy while coding, and refer to it often as you become more familiar with C's syntax and terminology.

www.ingramcontent.com/pod-product-compliance
Lightning Source LLC
Chambersburg PA
CBHW050000230526
45465CB00003BB/1184